Math[...] Games and[...]

Roy[...]

Senior Lecturer in Ma[...]
Dundee College of Educa[...]

Hart-Davis Educational

Granada Publishing Limited
Hart-Davis Educational Limited
First published 1971 by Chatto and Windus (Educational) Limited
Second edition published 1977 by Hart-Davis Educational Limited
Frogmore, St. Albans, Hertfordshire
Reprinted 1978, 1979, 1981

ISBN 0 247 12779 5
Printed in Great Britain by
Fletcher & Son Ltd, Norwich

Granada ®
Granada Publishing ®

Introduction

This book is intended for teachers of children with chronological ages ranging from five to thirteen years. Some of these children will have mental ages well below (or above) these limits.

The games and activities are particularly recommended to motivate and interest the less able pupils in primary and lower secondary schools. Many variations are suggested and teachers can adapt these to suit individual requirements.

The games can be used as starting-points and the teacher and the children can modify them freely. This will encourage a creative attitude that will greatly extend the scope of this book, and consequently add to its value.

An appreciation of why rules are needed in games, and in life, will be fostered, especially when the children change the rules. This involves co-operation and agreement and thus social values are developed alongside the mathematical ones.

A major aim is to provide for the interesting, enjoyable practising of existing skills, but needs will arise during the course of play that will motivate new learning. The games will supplement and enrich the normal school programme and provide mathematical experience of importance. The sort of competition involved is in no way detrimental as it does not involve the failure, anxiety and fear that are so often associated with competition in the classroom.

The materials needed are readily available in all schools and any apparatus required can be easily constructed by a teacher with no practical aptitude. Whenever possible the children themselves should make the apparatus. The games in this book have been thoroughly tested in schools.

In general the games increase in difficulty as one progresses through the book, but there are so many variations given that this ordering should only be regarded as a rough guide.

Paper and pencil are assumed always to be available and have not therefore been listed under Materials.

Older children is used in the sense of mental age rather than chronological age.

Number words refer to one, two, and so on.

Numbering, such as '1 to 10', is always inclusive.

1

Materials. Card.

Experiences to be gained. Counting; linking of number and the shapes of numerals.

The teacher draws the numerals each on a card of a different colour. They are then cut out and each numeral is divided into the same number of parts as the numeral represents.

The numeral five would therefore be divided into five parts as shown. The children construct the numerals and can count the component parts as a check.

Variations. The size of the component parts for each numeral could be equal in area. This would enable the parts to be allocated by comparing component sizes and colour could be abandoned, thus making the task more difficult but also more instructive.

2

Materials. Dominoes.

Experiences to be gained. Counting; recognition of patterns; addition.

The dominoes are placed face downwards on the table. One of them is turned over and the player calls out the two numbers represented by the spots. If many children are to be involved they can write down the numerals rather than await turns.

Home-made dominoes written on card, are to be preferred as the position of the spots can be varied. The all too frequent association of five with , and the consequent refusal of a child to accept  as five, is thus avoided.

A more advanced game could be used where the children call out, or write down, the total number of the two sets of spots on the domino turned over.

If a timing device is available a child can try to improve on the time he takes to name all the totals.

The teacher can check the results by asking the children to place the dominoes in a line and record their total each time.

3

Materials. Cups and saucers—preferably plastic ones as in a doll's set; lumps of sugar (peas or beans could be used to represent the sugar).

Experiences to be gained. 1–1 correspondence; conservation; estimation; counting; vocabulary—too many, too few.

This game is for the younger children. A child is shown some cups (say nine) and is asked to get some saucers so that there is one for each cup. The saucers (say fifteen) are best placed a fair distance from the cups so that a direct comparison is difficult.

The number of saucers should be greater than the number of cups as it is instructive to see if the child brings all the saucers or not.

If the child starts to count the cups he should be stopped, but praised for his quite correct approach to the problem. It should be explained that we want him to guess (estimate) how many saucers will be needed.

When the child returns with the saucers he should be asked to see if he has the right number or too many or too few. This may be done by counting or by 1–1 correspondence, where each cup is paired with each saucer.

Whichever method is used the child should be asked if he could do it another way. Some children can use 1–1 correspondence but not counting as a method, whereas others may use counting with no real understanding of the relationship between the two sets of objects that are counted, i.e. the fact that they can be paired without counting at all.

The teacher should ensure that the child appreciates the direct link between the number of saucers and cups, so that logically they understand the following relationships: $a = b$ and $c = b$ implies $a = c$. Naturally they would not be able to express it in this algebraic form but suitable questioning should reveal whether the idea involved has been established or not.

4

Materials. Cuisenaire rods.

Experiences to be gained. Estimating length.

The children draw round the Cuisenaire rods so as to produce sheets of rectangles.

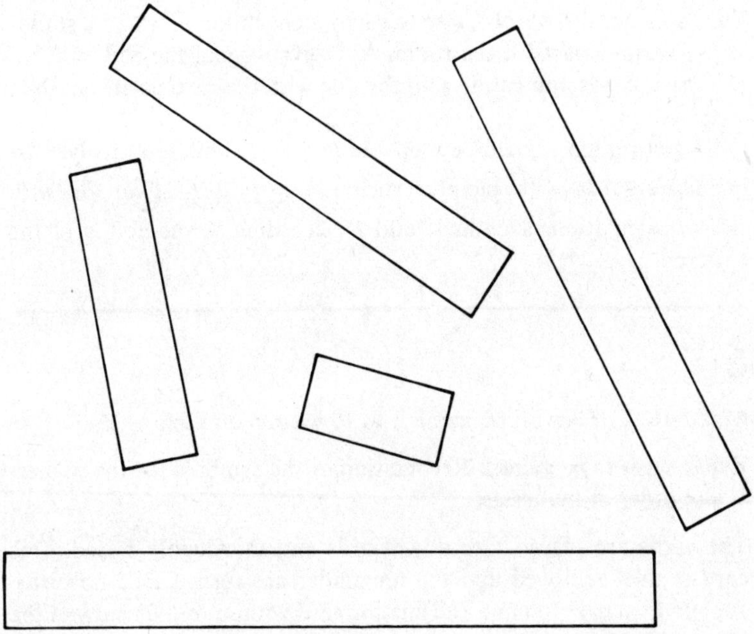

The sheets are now exchanged and the children fit rods onto the rectangles, the object being to do this in as few trials as possible.

5

Materials. Large cards with the numerals 1 to 5 written on them; others with words for the numerals on them, ONE, TWO, THREE, FOUR, FIVE.

Experiences to be gained. Recognition of the symbols and words for numerals.

The cards are distributed, one to each of ten children, who are standing in various parts of the room. At a given signal the children display their cards and run to join the one with the card corresponding to theirs.

Larger numbers could be used and also more children involved by including cards with pictures such as  or with simple calculations such as '1 add 2' according to the ability of the children.

6

Materials. Cards with numerals 1 to 10 written on them.

Experiences to be gained. Recognition of the symbols for the numerals; order of numerals.

The cards are placed face downwards and thoroughly mixed. One card is then removed and the remainder are turned face upwards. A child then tries to name the missing card without moving any of the others. If this proves too difficult they are allowed to rearrange the cards in any way they wish.

Variations can be introduced by replacing the numerals by pictures. For example the numeral 5 card might be replaced by a picture of five ducks or else a simple sum such as '2 add 3'.

7

Materials. A die with spots.

Experiences to be gained. 1–1 correspondence; counting.

Each player draws six beetles each with six legs. Two children play, each throwing the die in turn. Depending on the number of spots shown the player fills in the corresponding number of legs. The teacher can draw the beetles for very young children and even if they cannot count they can fill in the legs by 1–1 correspondence, one leg for each spot on the die.

The first player to fill in all the legs wins.

If the numbers are to be kept to five and less, a child's building brick can be used and the numbers 1 to 5 and an extra 1 written on it in chalk; alternatively the six spot on the die could be covered with paper and one spot drawn.

Children object to one face being left blank (and also to having one marked 0) so one spot will appear on two faces.

Variations such as adding eyes, wings, etc., can be used so as to introduce larger numbers. These could be varied in value and should be indicated on a 'key beetle' so as to avoid burdening the memory.

8

Materials. Twenty cards (four colours should be used so that there are five cards of each colour). The five cards have the numerals 1, 2, 3, 4 and 5 written on them.

Experiences to be gained. Classifying by colour; order of the numerals.

Four children play but by modifying the number of cards used the game can be adapted for any number of children. (The number of cards should be five times the number of children; seven children would need thirty-five cards, i.e. 1, 2, 3, 4 and 5 in seven colours.)

The cards are shuffled and the first player puts down a card with 1 on it if he can. Suppose this card is red, then the next player can put down a red 2 or else start a new column with a 1.

The play can be illustrated by considering one stage of a game, in which we will suppose the colours to be red, blue, yellow and green.

Red 1	Blue 1	Yellow 1
Red 2	Blue 2	
	Blue 3	

The next player could play a red 3, a blue 4, a yellow 2 or a green 1.

A larger number of cards could be used and another variation is to start with the middle numeral instead of 1. In the case above they would start with 3 and the next player could then follow with a 2 or a 4 or 3 in another colour.

9

Materials. None.

Experiences to be gained. Sequence of numerals; straight lines.

This game is for the younger children. The teacher draws a shape consisting of straight lines and numbers the vertices in order.

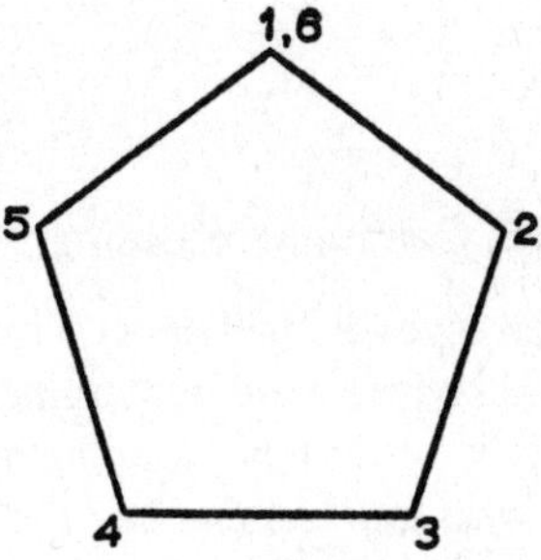

By using tracing paper five numbered points are made, the joining lines being omitted. These are left for the children to join. The children can then be given examples, with some details already completed.

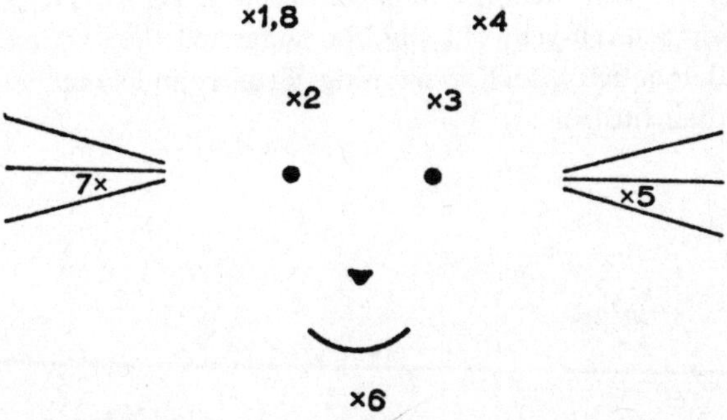

After sufficient experiences of this kind the children should construct their own puzzles on these lines. Older children can devise a method of indicating the extra details, such as the whiskers, eyes, nose and mouth shown above. The numerals might, for example, be listed with a stroke / between sets that are not to be joined. Another way would be to show each connected set in a different colour.

10

Materials. None.

Experiences to be gained. Counting; recording.

The number of children involved will depend on the counting ability of the group. Each child is given a different number and another member of the class then claps her hands, stopping at one of the numbers allocated. The person with that number can then do the clapping for the next number.

If numbers are called only once, more children will get a turn and there is the additional advantage that a method of recording will be required. This should be suggested and operated by the children.

For variety the numbers given to the children could be changed frequently thus introducing complications if each child is to be sure of a turn. Some seven-year-old children suggested they should get on with another activity, such as painting, jig-saws and so on, when they had had their turn.

11

Materials. Thick card; pegs.

Experiences to be gained. Linking the numerals to the corresponding numbers.

The numerals 1 to 9 are cut out of card. Holes are cut so that the pegs will just fit in them; the number of holes corresponds to the numeral so that 3 has three holes in it, 6 has six holes and so on.

For example:

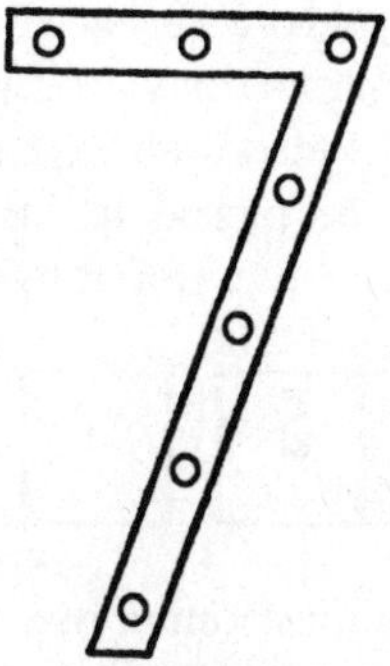

12

Materials. Two sets of cards each with numerals written on them; counters or building bricks.

Experiences to be gained. Recognition of numerals and matching them with the appropriate number of counters.

Two teams are lined up and a set of cards, well mixed, is placed in front of each team, but at the other end of the room. At a given signal the first child from each team runs to collect the top card, places the number of counters on it according to the numeral indicated, and then returns to his team and touches the next member of the team.

The process is repeated and the first team to finish wins provided no mistakes have been made.

13

Materials. Card.

Experiences to be gained. Recognition and matching of numbers represented by numerals, words and pictures.

Rectangles are cut out of card, 6 cm by 3 cm being a convenient size. A thick line is drawn down the middle of each rectangle so as to divide it into two squares. Dominoes are now made by writing numerals, number words or pictures, e.g. 3, THREE and 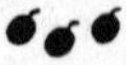 respectively. The latter should be varied and not merely be spots or arranged in the traditional positions used on dominoes. Simple calculations could also be included if desired, such as 3 add 2, 4 – 1, etc.

The dominoes should be placed in line and the two end ones matched by constructing another domino, if necessary.

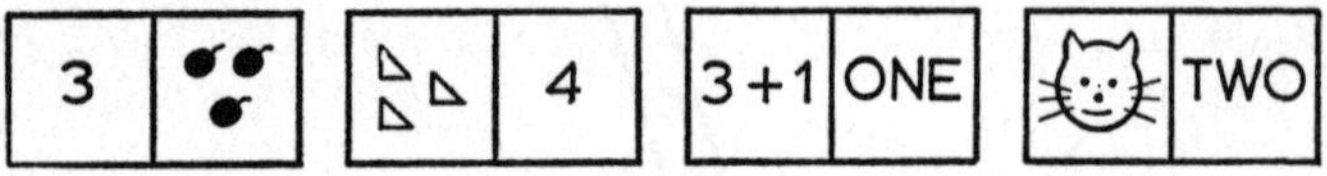

In the case above a domino containing, say 2 and THREE would produce the required matching. The players should be allowed to play their dominoes upside-down if they wish.

Each player places a domino in turn provided part of it matches one of the ends of the line so far formed. If a player cannot do this he misses that turn. The first player left without any dominoes is the winner, but if no one can go then the one with the least dominoes in his hand wins.

If the children can add up all the numbers represented on the dominoes they have left then this can be used to determine the winner, i.e. the one whose total is least.

Other variations can be obtained by modifying games 22 and 41. Shape dominoes could be used so that children recognize and match figures with the same number of sides but different shapes.

14

Materials. A box; card; counters, beads or peas.

Experiences to be gained. Counting; number bonds.

A rectangular piece of card is folded into a wedge shape so that it will fit into the box as shown.

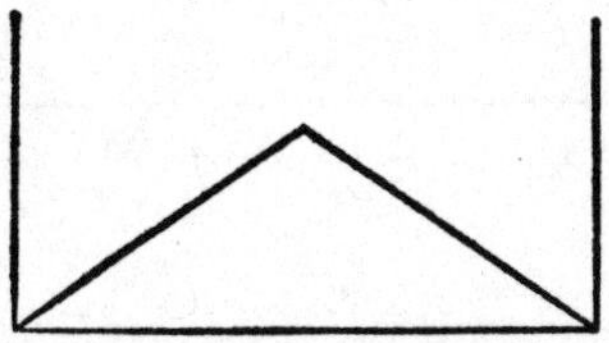

Small objects such as beads are dropped onto the ridge so that some fall on one side and some on the other. If a child needs practice in the number bonds of eight, for instance, they can be given eight beads to drop.

Recording the results will facilitate checking and has an important role to play after some initial verbal work.

15

Materials. Card.

Experiences to be gained. Shape; angle and line relationships.

Each child cuts out a figure; this can be a square, rectangle, triangle, circle pattern or it could represent a person or animal. The figures are then cut into a number of pieces, exchanged and then re-assembled.

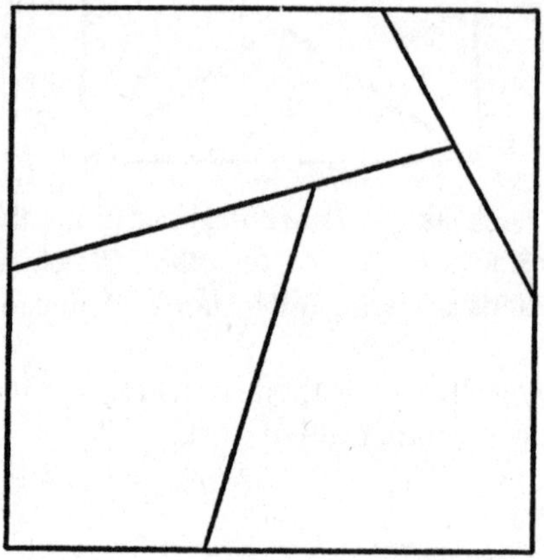

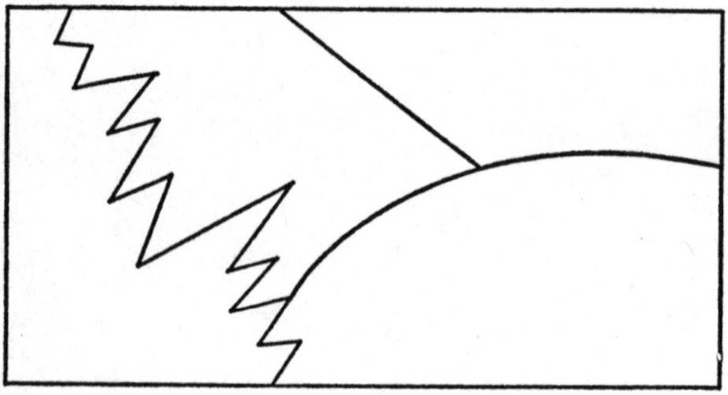

Extensions and modifications of this work will appear in tessellations, tangrams and jig-saws.

16

Materials. Counters of different colours, one for each player; a die.

Experiences to be gained. Counting; addition; subtraction.

A strip of paper is cut out so as to form a road and nineteen sections are marked on it. Graph paper could be used.

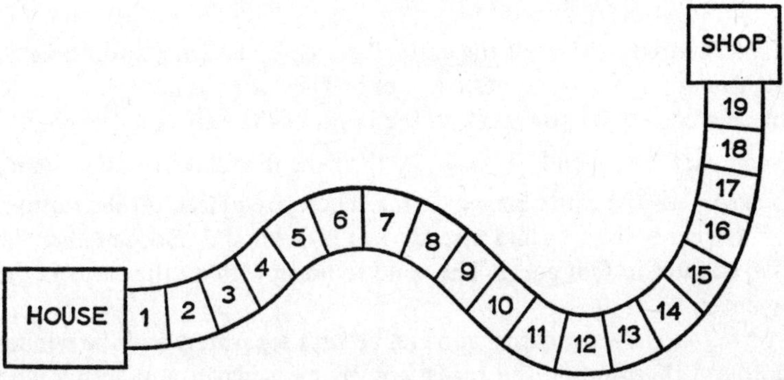

Each player throws the die in turn and moves his own counter according to the numeral on the die face.

The first player to reach the shop wins and this will represent a total score of twenty.

To introduce subtraction a player may move his counter forward on his first two throws and backwards on the third one.

As the first player has an advantage the players should take it in turns to throw first. Using a number larger than twenty reduces the effect of having the first throw.

17

Materials. Sets of cards all the same size. The numerals, pictures, number words and simple operations (e.g. $2 + 3$) are written one on each card. The size of the numbers used will depend on the age and ability of the children.

Experiences to be gained. Matching in pairs of any two of the following—numerals, pictures, number words or simple operations.

Two children divide out the cards between them using two, three or all four of the sets suggested above. They then take it in turn to place a card, face upwards, on the table. If the pair of cards correspond, e.g. $2 + 1$ and △ △ △ then the first child to say, 'Snap', picks up all the cards played so far. These are placed on the bottom of the cards that a child already has in her hand and can then be played later in that game. The child to finish with all the cards is the winner.

Alternatively any cards won can be kept separately and the winner is found by counting the cards won by each player and seeing who has the most.

18

Materials. Cuisenaire rods.

Experiences to be gained. Estimation of length and number; use of units, multiplication; commutativity.

A child is asked to take any number of rods from the box, but they must all be the same colour. He should estimate how many he has taken and check this by counting. The rods are arranged to form a rectangle as shown below, where five blue rods were chosen.

The child now selects a rod that he thinks will fit exactly across the five blue rods. He checks his selection and changes it if incorrect, thus exercising his estimating powers which will improve with these experiences. When a yellow rod has been correctly selected the child should be asked to estimate how many he will need altogether to fit on top of the blue rods.

Suppose he thinks eight will be needed. He should be asked to pick up, without first counting, what he thinks will be eight yellow rods. This can then be checked by counting the rods as they are placed on the blue ones. Since nine are needed he will need to take one more and this will lead to improvement in his estimations of both number and length.

By using a white rod as the unit the five blue ones can be seen to be equivalent to forty-five units and similarly the nine yellow rods could be replaced by forty-five units. This can therefore give rise to multiplication $9 \times 5 = 5 \times 9 = 45$, and the commutative law $a \times b = b \times a$.

19

Materials. A board; hooks; quoits (these can be made from rope or thick string).

Experiences to be gained. Counting; addition; subtraction; one-to-one correspondence; recording.

The size of the board, hooks and quoits will depend on the throwing skills of the children and on the distance they stand from the board. The board can be divided into any required number of sections with one hook in each.

Numerals should not be written in each section unless the children should suggest this. As with other games of this type young children object to two different scores for actions they consider to be of equal difficulty.

Counting will be practised when taking an agreed number of quoits and in finding out the number that stay on the hooks. The scores can be recorded each time and added at the end of a session of games; the player with the greater score wins. Alternatively the difference between the scores of the two players could be recorded. This would give practice in subtracting mentally. Teams could be used or a knock-out competition organized.

For very young children the scores could be recorded by one-to-one correspondence, each child making one stroke on paper for each quoit that is thrown on to a hook.

20

Materials. Rulers; string; balls.

Experiences to be gained. Horizontal; vertical.

Two rulers, edges uppermost, are held apart by two objects at their ends. They are tied or held in position by sellotape and a ball placed on the ruler so that it can run horizontally along the edges.

A more permanent structure could be made with four pieces of wood nailed together. A marble between two pencils will provide a simple alternative.

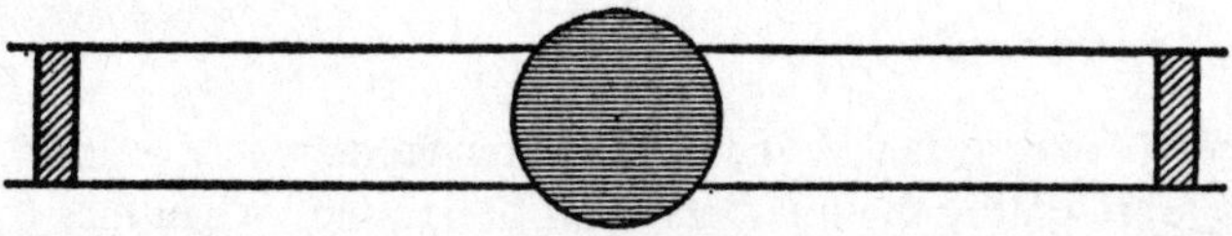

The apparatus can be used to see whether surfaces are horizontal or not. This can be conveniently combined with the use of a plumb line, made by hanging a small heavy object from a piece of thin string. In this way the horizontal and the vertical can be linked together and the right angle relationship noted. As a separate check the children can test for right angles as described in Number 32.

21

Materials. Ten cards with pictures and ten cards with numerals both sets representing the numbers from one to ten. When face downwards all the cards should be indistinguishable.

Experiences to be gained. Matching the picture cards to those with the corresponding numerals. Notion of position, thus laying the foundation for future simple co-ordinate work.

The cards are placed face downwards and thoroughly mixed. They are then arranged in orderly rows and columns, for example, four rows with five cards in each.

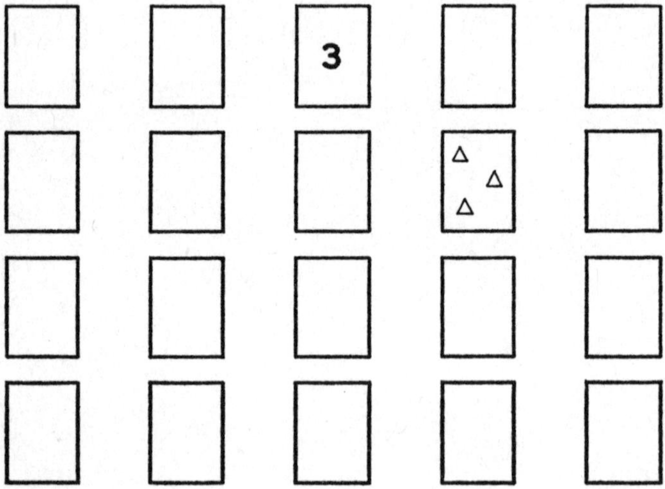

The first player turns over two cards. If they match he keeps them but if they do not match they are replaced, face downwards.

The player who finishes with the larger number of cards is the winner. Questions as to which rows and columns cards are in will help children to develop elementary co-ordinate ideas, e.g. 1st row, 2nd column. For the more able children the results could be recorded, 3, 4 would represent the 3rd column and the 4th row thus denoting the card marked 3 in the diagram.

22

Materials. Cards with the names of the numerals written on them; one, two, three and so on according to the ability of the children concerned.

Experiences to be gained. Linking of the numeral names to the corresponding symbol, e.g. six → 6.

One of the name cards is shown to the children and they write down the symbol. This can be modified by showing cards with the symbol on and the children writing down its name.

Similarly instructions such as '3 add 4' could be used if practice with number bonds is desired.

23

Materials. Cardboard; paper clips or fasteners; string; a rod.

Experiences to be gained. Counting; addition; subtraction; time; recording.

Fishes about 5 to 8 cm long are cut out of cardboard and a steel paper clip or fastener attached to each. A magnet attached to a line is used to fish with and after a given time the child counts how many fish have been caught. Other children can be allowed the same amount of time, say one minute, and this provides real experience of how long a minute is.

By comparing scores subtraction can be introduced and a team competition would involve addition. The need to record the scores arises naturally when several children are playing. Two or more fishing pools could be used and this eliminates the need for timing.

The practice of putting numbers on the fish is not to be recommended as children regard it as unfair when two fish are caught that are the same size yet one counts for more than the other. The number on the fish, say 3, is in no way associated with 'one and one and one', the cardinal aspect of the number, so if different values are to be used the size of the fish should be varied according to the size of the number on it.

A more elaborate scheme with metal fish could be used so that the children could weigh them and allocate scores accordingly. All the weights used would then need to be exact multiples of weights of the lightest fish.

24

Materials. A card about 10 cm by 10 cm; drawing pins; thin ribbon, wool or string; cards with one numeral written on each.

Experiences to be gained. Recognition and linking of the symbols and written words representing the numerals.

The card is divided into sections and the words for the numerals written in these sections.

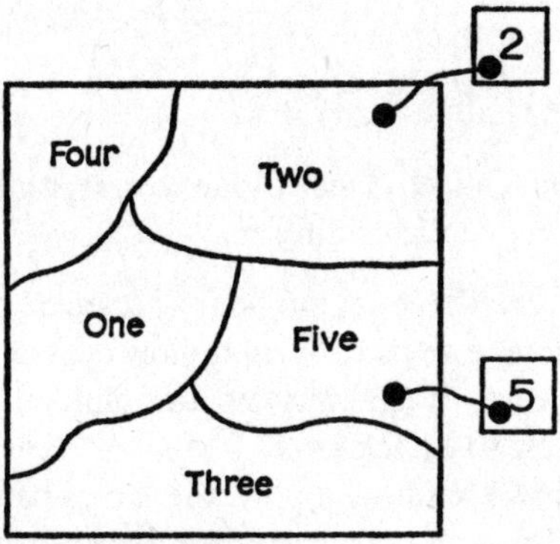

A length of ribbon is attached to each of five drawing pins. A child closes his eyes and sticks a drawing pin into the card. He then uses another drawing pin to fix the free end of the ribbon to the corresponding card, for example FIVE and 5, TWO and 2 (see diagram.)

Simple number combinations or pictures could be used instead of one set of cards, so that the corresponding pairs might be 3 + 1 and 4 or △ △ △ and 2 + 1.

25

Materials. Skittles; ball.

Experiences to be gained. One-to-one correspondence; counting; addition; subtraction; recording.

If skittles are not available rectangular cards can be rolled and the edges held by sellotape so as to form hollow cylinders. This gives the additional experience of stability as the children discover which cylinders are easiest to knock over.

Two players or two teams can play, the scores being recorded after every throw, or else each player can be allowed two or three throws before he counts how many skittles he has knocked over.

Very young children can make a tally by putting a mark on paper for every skittle knocked over. If the opponent makes his marks under those of the first player they can keep a running total by noting the excess of one over the other. This one-to-one correspondence method keeps the number low, and permits simple counting. Terms such as 'more than', 'less than', 'fewer than', and so on will occur.

If the skittles are numbered the level of difficulty can be made more appropriate for older children, but as mentioned in the fishing game (23) young children regard it as unfair to get different scores for knocking over similar skittles. This can to some extent be allowed for by making the skittles different sizes, weights or varying their distances, but the final verdict on the fairness of the game should be left to the children.

26

Materials. Fifteen cards. Five with one numeral on each, 1, 2, 3, 4 and 5. Five with the words for the numerals written on them—ONE, TWO, etc. Five pictures of objects to illustrate the number involved (e.g. ).

Experiences to be gained. Matching numerals, words and pictures.

This game is for three children, but by varying the number of cards it can easily be adapted for larger groups. The cards once mixed are then dealt. The object is to collect all five cards in any one of the three sets mentioned—numerals, words or pictures.

Each child selects a card they do not wish to keep and when they have all done this one of them gives the order to PASS. The unwanted cards are all passed to the left (or the right if that is agreed upon). This process is continued until someone has a completed set.

If five children play the aim could be changed so that they collect three corresponding cards, for example

2, TWO and .

With little or no modification 'Snap' and other games mentioned elsewhere could also be played with these cards (see Numbers 5, 6, 8, 17).

27

Materials. Counters; a bag or box.

Experiences to be gained. Number bonds; odd and even numbers.

Any number of children can play. To illustrate the game we will suppose practice is needed in the numbers that add up to nine. Nine counters, or other small objects, are placed in the bag and a child takes out some of them and shows these to another child. Let us assume he sees three counters; he must then say how many counters remain in the bag and, if he is correct, he scores one point. The children take turns to say how many there will be or else they can all be asked to write down their forecast. The latter method is preferable as more children are directly involved in the play.

A variation of this game can be used to develop an appreciation of odd and even numbers. In the above example, using nine counters, the children could record their results and discover that if an even number is removed an odd number remains, and if an odd number is removed then an even number remains. The investigation of numbers other than nine could then follow.

28

Materials. Pegboard and pegs.

Experiences to be gained. Estimation, 1–1 correspondence; too many; too few.

An area is traced in chalk on some pegboard. The children then take as many pegs as they think will be necessary to fill all the holes enclosed by the chalk line.

Each child places the pegs into the holes and thus finds out if they have too many or too few. This result is noted and the one whose estimate was nearest is the winner.

The older children can also be asked to state the number of pegs they think will be required, as opposed to just picking up as many as they think they need.

29

Materials. Chalk; string; bean bags.

Experiences to be gained. Throwing accuracy; idea of distances; counting; adding; subtraction; recording.

A circle is drawn by tying a stick of chalk to one end of a piece of string, holding the other end at a fixed point and tracing out the circle. A radius of half a metre is convenient. Children stand behind a line about 3 to 4 metres from the centre of the circle and throw bean bags, or other suitable objects, into the circle. The bags should be in two different colours, one for each child, or else marked so that the children can tell which ones they threw.

By playing several games, and scoring a point for each bag that remains in the circle, counting, adding and the need for recording emerge. Comparing individual or team scores provides subtraction experience or matching 1–1 and seeing if there are any left over if children are at the pre-counting stage.

Variations can be made in the shape and size of the target, several circles used (with the same centre) or the target placed near a wall so that rebounding is considered. Objects that can be rolled can be used instead of objects to be thrown.

30

Materials. A variety of objects (see below).

Experiences to be gained. Classifying.

A number of objects are presented and the children have to decide what they have in common. For example, there might be a red brick, spoon, twig, peg and a box that are all made of wood. In another game the objects might all contain a circle in some form or other, e.g. a coin, cylindrical container, ball and ring.

Groups of children can collect such sets of objects and display them in turn on a table so that the other children can find the common property.

31

Materials. Wire; beads; cane.

Experiences to be gained. Counting; number bonds.

Beads are threaded on the wire the ends of which are pushed into a piece of garden cane, or wood with two suitable holes made in it. The holes can be made with a nail so that the ends of the wire fit firmly into them.

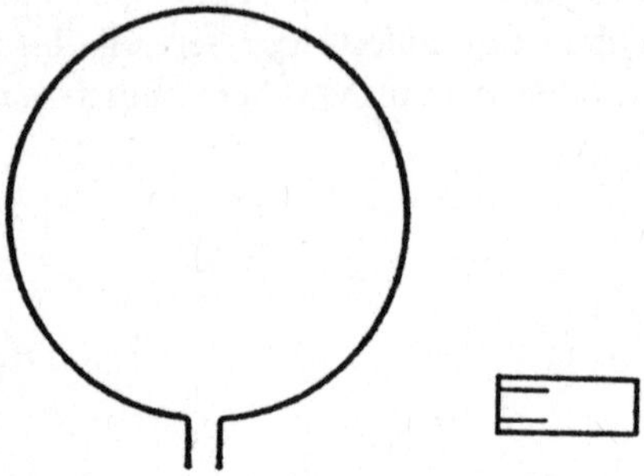

By shaking the wire some beads go to one side and some to the other. If, for example practice in the number bonds for seven are required the seven beads on successive shakes may be partitioned (6,1), (3,4), (5,2), (2,5) and so on. After dealing with the work verbally recording can be introduced, and it can then be ensured that all the possible bonds have been adequately experienced.

The flexible arrangement suggested allows the number of beads on the wire to be varied, but a more permanent structure could be made with the wire fixed to the handle. In this case more of these 'number bats' will be needed with a different number of beads on each.

32

Materials. Paper.

Experiences to be gained. Paper folding; straight line; right angle.

Each child is provided with a piece of paper with no straight edges.

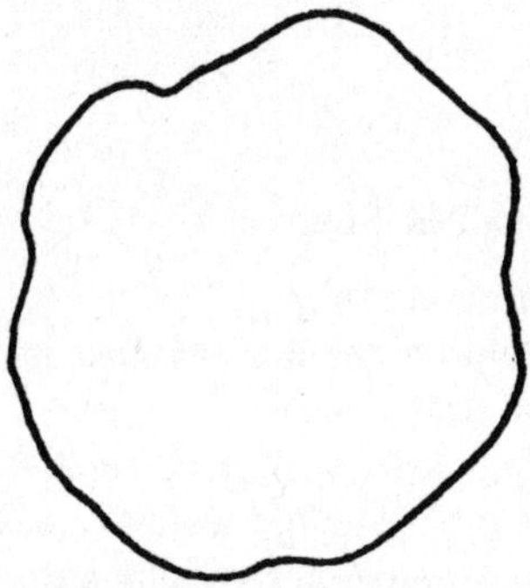

(a)

They are asked to produce a straight line, using nothing but the paper. When this has been done (by folding) the children will each have some such figure as below

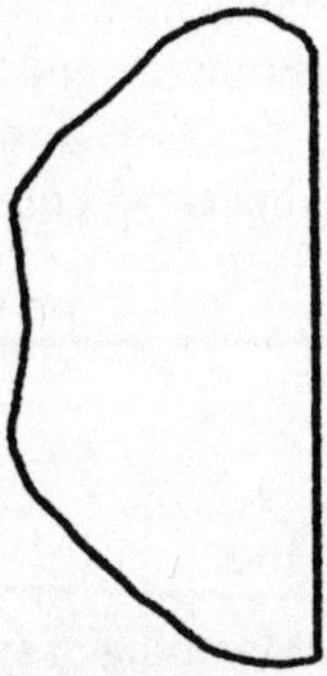

(b)

They are then asked to make a right angle, the term having been introduced via the many examples that exist in the environment—windows, books, tables, etc.

The figure, produced by folding the line in (b) back on top of itself, can then be used to test for right angles, the objects containing them being listed if desired.

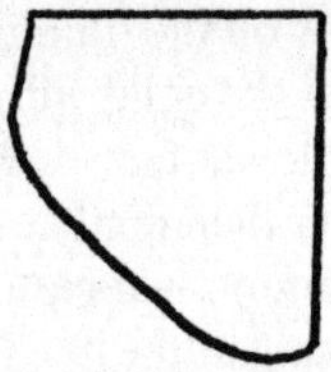

(c)

33

Materials. Card.

Experiences to be gained. Shapes.

Any number of children can play.

Suppose the children require practice in recognizing rectangles, circles, squares and triangles.

The four words could be written on separate cards and placed face downwards on the table. A child selects one of them, say a rectangle, and has to give an example of that shape that is in the classroom. If she chooses 'the top of a book' to illustrate a rectangle, then later answers, such as 'the bottom of a book' or 'a page in a book' can be rejected if the teacher wishes. (Better still, a panel of children could be appointed to adjudicate in such matters.)

Objects outside the classroom could also be permitted.

A similar game could be played using cube, cuboid, sphere and cylinder. The words introduced will obviously depend on the age and ability of the children.

34

Materials. A set of dominoes.

Experiences to be gained. Matching of spot patterns.

(a) The normal game can be played with the dominoes distributed amongst the players, any remaining ones being set aside. The player with the double six plays first and then the player on his left and so on. If a player cannot match the spots at either end of the line he takes one from the ones that were set aside.

When one player has used all his dominoes the others count the number of spots on the dominoes they have not yet played. After several games the child with the lowest total wins.

(b) One domino is removed face downwards so that the spots are not seen. The player then matches the dominoes as in (a) above and the missing domino will match the spots at the ends of the line. Thus the forming of the line is easily checked by the player.

35

Materials. A collection of small toys, bricks, pencils and other objects varying in colour and in the material they are made of.

Experiences to be gained. Classifying.

None of the objects should contain more than one colour and the material they are made of should be discussed with the children. Suppose three colours are used, red, black and yellow. The materials might be plastic, wood and metal.

One child thinks of an object and the rest of the group can ask one question each in turn. The question must be such that it can be answered by YES or NO and if it cannot be answered in this way the child thinking of the object refuses to answer. The aim is for the group to determine what the object is in as few questions as possible. Some children may ask questions such as, 'Are you thinking of this green pencil?' but this direct method is inefficient. 'Is it yellow?' and 'Is it made of plastic?' will produce quicker results in general.

The game will prove unsatisfactory unless the children have been given practice in classifying by partitioning the sets according to colour, then by material and similarly by any other criterion available, e.g. 'has wheels'.

36

Materials. A set of dominoes.

Experiences to be gained. Addition; subtraction; number bonds.

A number is agreed upon, say eight. The player with the double six places that on the table and the next player puts down a domino making the total of those touching eight. For example.

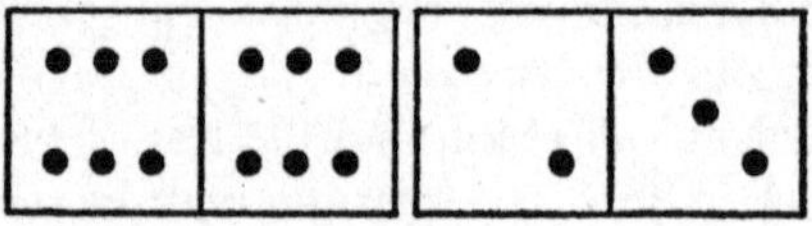

The following player will now need to find a domino with two spots to go on the left or else one with five spots to place on the right.

One point can be scored for the player who first gets rid of all his dominoes or else the total spots can be counted on remaining dominoes and the one with the lowest final score becomes the winner. If the first of these is used it may happen that no player is able to get rid of all his dominoes and the one with the least number of dominoes remaining is then the winner.

37

Materials. Graph paper; counters.

Experiences to be gained. Counting; odd and even numbers.

The game as described is for two players. A strip of graph paper, of any agreed length, is used and each player places a counter in any one of the squares.

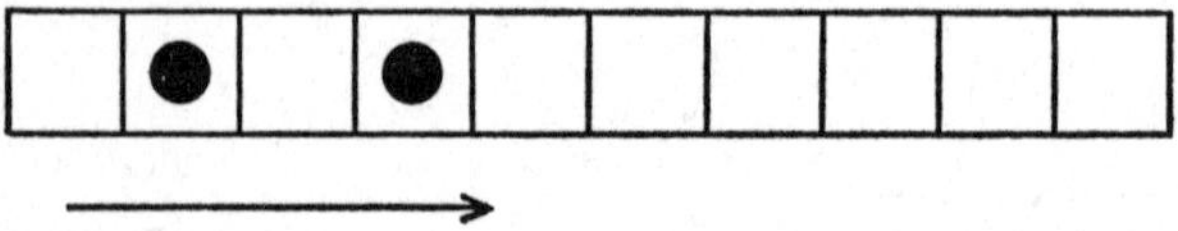

The first player can move either counter one square to the right; the second player has a similar choice and play proceeds alternately. When a counter reaches the last square it is removed. The player who moves the last counter is the winner.

Two counters can be on the same square at once, unless agreed otherwise by the players.

Variations could involve more players, each playing in turn with the two counters as above, or more counters could be introduced. It is not essential to have the same number of counters as there are players.

The children should suggest their own modifications, such as moving two squares each time, jumping over other counters, a choice of moving one or two squares, the right not to move at all once in a game and so on.

38

Materials. Graph paper or card.

Experiences to be gained. Addition; subtraction; multiplication; division; recording.

Rectangles (2 cm by 4 cm is a convenient size) are cut out of card or graph paper and two numbers written on them, for example, [4,2]. Other cards are provided with the totals on them, in this case [6]. The children pair them off so as to get practice in addition and if required can record their work in the form, $4,2 \xrightarrow{add} 6$. This method can be adapted for other number operations. The equals sign with its many difficulties is avoided.

Children can then make up their own questions and vary the method of presentation.

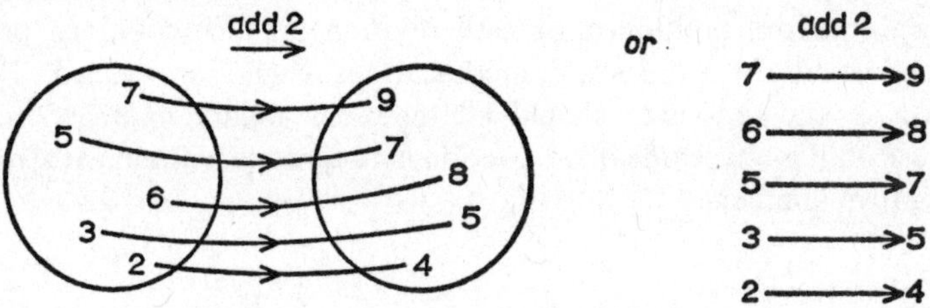

Reversing the arrows will lead to discussion of the inverse operation, in the above subtraction.

39

Materials. Cards in two different colours, say red and blue.

Experiences to be gained. Number bonds.

Numerals are written on both sets of cards. Any numerals will do but let us suppose practice is needed with addition bonds for the numbers 1 to 10. The cards are placed in two piles, each consisting of cards that are all the same colour. The cards in each pile are now mixed and placed beside each other, face upwards.

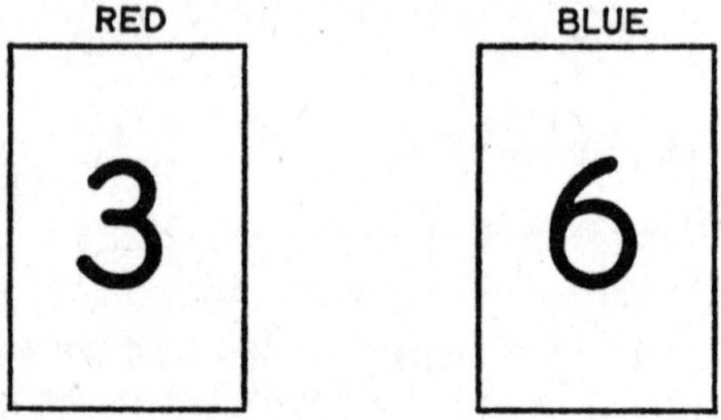

The child states the sum of the two numbers showing and then places the two cards on one side. If several children are playing they can agree on whether each answer is correct or not, the teacher being available to settle differences of opinion. Alternatively the child can write down each answer thus gaining experiences of recording.

Cards could be provided in a third colour, so that in the case above a yellow card with 9 on it might be selected and placed by the side of the 3 and 6.

Subtraction, multiplication and division practice could be provided similarly but certain modifications would be needed. For instance the red cards should all represent greater numbers than those on the blue cards if subtraction is to be done without involving negative numbers.

40

Materials. Pegboard; pegs; chalk.

Experiences to be gained. Odd and even; half.

An area is marked out on the pegboard with chalk. The game is described for two players but can be adapted for more. The players place a peg in turn until the area marked has been filled. The last player to put in a peg wins.

Young children should, after preliminary play, be encouraged to use a single line and then a simple rectangle with a width that will take two pegs. These experiences will lay a foundation for odd and even numbers and halving.

The older children will be able to forecast who will win when rectangles are used and, in some cases, with more complicated figures. A bonus point could be given to the first player to forecast who will win, and if he proves incorrect the extra point goes to his opponent.

When three players are involved a rectangle with a width that takes three pegs will be an important case to investigate and similarly for multiples of three. Varying the number of players will produce different cases and widen the experiences. Irregular figures will provide interesting problems for the most able children.

41

Materials. Dominoes.

Experiences to be gained. Addition; subtraction.

The dominoes are placed face downwards upon the table and any two of them are turned over.

The player records the result, e.g. (3+2) + (2+4), or (3,2) (2,4) or any other meaningful way. This can then be extended to give the total, (3+2) + (2+4) → (5+6) → 11. The use of the equal sign is not recommended except for the older children. They should be encouraged to record their results in a variety of ways and not restrict themselves to the two illustrations above.

By placing the domino with the larger number of spots on the left subtraction can be introduced. Only the older and most able children will be able to cope with the negative numbers that arise from accepting any order of the two dominoes.

Extensions involving three or more dominoes can provide larger numbers if required.

42

Materials. A number line; die; counters.

Experiences to be gained. Counting; addition; subtraction; preparation for negative numbers.

The numerals are written on both sides of the starting point (S.P.) which can be denoted by 0 if desired. The numerals on the right can be written in black ink and those on the left in red.

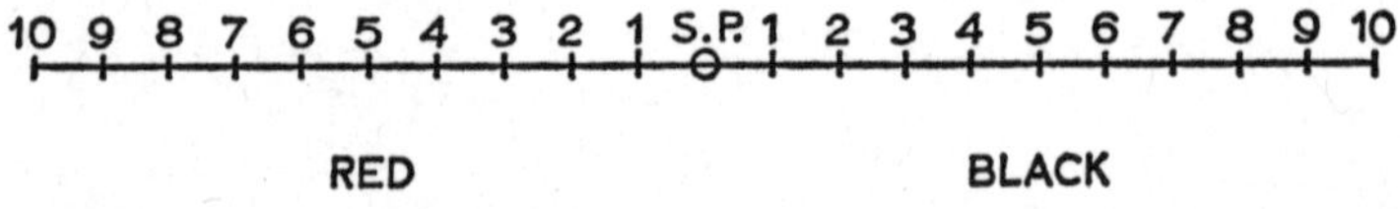

Any number of children can play; each has a counter of a different colour. These counters are placed at S.P. (or 0) and each player throws twice. The first throw shows how many places he is to move his counter to the right; the second throw indicates how many places it is to be moved to the left.

The two moves can be made separately or combined into one move. For example, if a player throws 3 and then 5 he can place his counter directly on the red 2 or else move it to the black 3 and then count five places to the left from there.

43

Materials. A die; counters.

Experiences to be gained. Counting; addition; subtraction.

Simple number bonds are written in spaces as shown below.

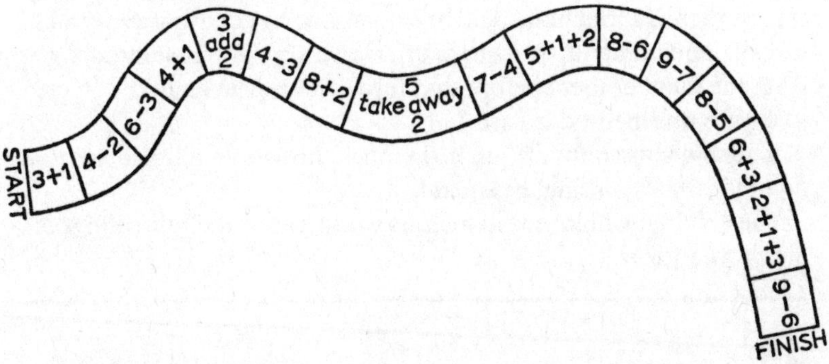

There is no restriction on the number of players, but each should have a counter of a different colour. The players throw the die in turn and the number of spots indicates how many spaces they can move; the move is not made unless the questions in all the spaces involved are answered correctly. For example, if a player at the start throws a three he moves his counter to the first space and states the answer, four, then to the second and answers two and finally to the third if he correctly states three. If he gave an incorrect first answer he would stay at the start, if wrong in answering the second question he would stay at the first space and if incorrect in the third answer he would stay at the second space. Briefly—he leaves his counter on the last one that he answered correctly.

44

Materials. Tennis balls; plastic balls.

Experiences to be gained. Counting; addition; subtraction; recording.

A square drawn with chalk, its sides 1 metre long, has some tennis balls placed in it. Children then roll or throw the plastic balls and try to knock the tennis balls out of the square.

Each child's score can be totalled and then compared with that of another. For younger children the numbers can be kept small by rolling alternately and only recording the difference. For example if A scores 4 and B scores 2 then A records 2 points in his favour.

The rules can be flexible. For example all the balls could be replaced after each throw or they could be re-set after, say, three throws each. Subtraction could be emphasized by counting the number of balls remaining in the square after each throw and subtracting it from the number there before that throw. (A screen could be erected to ensure this method is used.)

If tennis balls only are used the ones thrown could also score a point if they stay inside the square.

The children will invent numerous variations in the rules and scoring procedures.

45

Materials. Coloured pencils.

Experiences to be gained. Concept of relation; vocabulary.

Each arrow stands for the RELATION 'is larger than'.

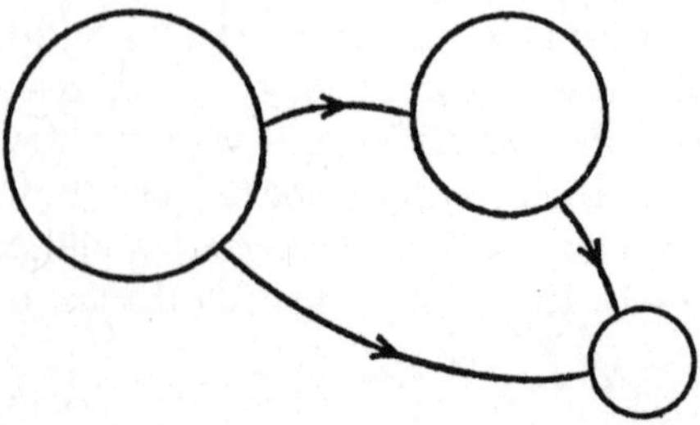

The arrows are on lines joining a larger circle to a smaller one.

The children draw three children of different heights. They can then join them by lines with arrows to show the relation 'is taller than'. On the same drawings a different-coloured pencil could be used to show 'is shorter than'.

The children can make up some more drawings and write at the top what the relation is, for example 'is fatter than', 'is heavier than', 'costs more than'. They can then exchange drawings with each other and put in the arrows. If they cannot agree as to whether they are correct or not then the teacher can join in the discussion and adjudicate.

46

Materials. Card.

Experiences to be gained. Addition; subtraction; probability.

This game is for two players. Both players have a set of nine cards, each with a different numeral, from 1 to 9, written on it. The players (A and B) then choose a number. Suppose A chooses 6 and B 12.

Each set of cards is mixed and placed, face downwards, in front of the players. They alternately turn a card over and if at any time the two cards add up to a chosen number then that player wins the cards already played. This could easily be modified so that the two numbers on the cards are subtracted.

In each case the children should develop an increasing awareness that some results are more probable than others.

Twenty would obviously be a poor choice and so would any number greater than eight in the subtraction variation.

Which numbers would be best to choose?

47

Materials. Graph paper or geo-board.

Experiences to be gained. Left, right; compass directions; recording.

A square is drawn and sub-divided as shown. The lines are regarded

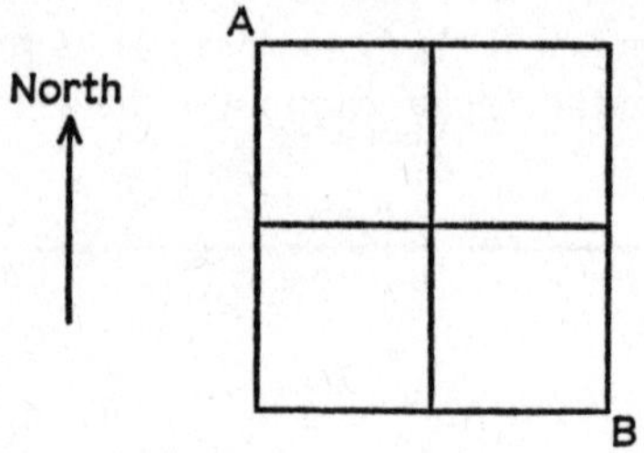

as roads and the problem is to find how many ways you can travel from A to B, if you do not go along any road twice in any one journey.

The problem could be simplified by adding the condition that you must never travel North or West. The use of compass directions is in no way essential, but is used here to make the explanation easier. Down and up and left and right appear frequently in children's work on this problem, but many record their results by drawings using arrows and/or coloured pencils.

48

Materials. None.

Experiences to be gained. Spatial ideas.

The children draw a series of maps of the form shown below, or else duplicated sheets can be provided. The size and number of divisions can be varied from child to child.

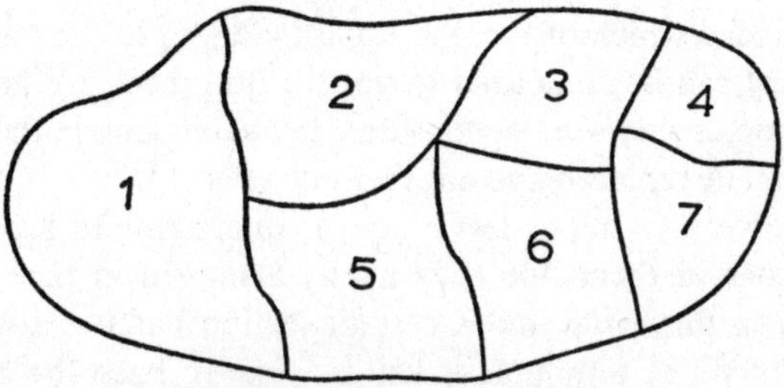

We will assume the figure represents an island that is divided into a number of regions which we will call counties.

The object is to colour the counties so that no two which are touching have the same colour. Young children often solve this by simply using different colours for each county; they can then be asked to use as few colours as possible.

Two counties can be in the same colour if they meet a point (e.g. 6 and 2 in the diagram) but not if they have a line in common. 2 cannot be the same colour as 3, but can be the same as 4. Not more than four colours are needed for any map.

49

Materials. Cuisenaire rods.

Experiences to be gained. Estimating and comparison of length, visually and by touch.

The ten different rods are placed on the table. A child places its hands behind its back and is given a rod to hold. It can be felt but not looked at; in this way it is compared with the rods on the table. Having decided which of them is equal in length to the one they are holding they can be compared by touch. Both rods are held behind the back, and, if they are not considered equal in length, the rod from the table can be replaced and another one selected.

With the very young or less able it is interesting to leave the box open in front of them, the rods neatly arranged in their compartments. When they note that a certain section has two rods missing from it, instead of only one, it will be time to keep the box out of sight when choosing which rod to give them.

Variations. Place the ten different rods on the table and mix them. Remove one when a child is not looking and then ask him which has been removed. If this proves too difficult they can rearrange them in order; should they not do this the game can be started with the rods ordered and then one removed.

In another game a child, blindfolded, could be asked to find which of the ten rods is missing.

50

Materials. Card in three different colours.

Experiences to be gained. Classifying by several criteria; vocabulary.

A large triangle, circle, square and rectangle are cut out in each of three colours, which we will suppose to be red, yellow and blue. Similarly small figures are cut out in each shape and colour mentioned, so that there will be twenty-four figures altogether.

Preliminary discussion can establish how many of these figures are (a) large, (b) small, (c) yellow, (d) four sided, (e) circles and so on.

This could in itself be used as the basis of a game with two teams, each member asking a question in turn that must be answered by his opposite number.

For the main game one child thinks of a particular figure, for example a large red square.

Questions are asked by the other children in turn and these are counted, for the object is to find what figure has been thought of, but using as few questions as possible. Questions are only answered if this can be done by YES or NO. Broad questions such as, 'Is it large?' will prove more effective than particular ones such as, 'Is it a small blue square?' It is important that such strategies are left for the children to discover and not taught.

The following variation is useful when analysing the progress of individual children. One figure is removed when the child is not looking and he then has to find out all the details of that figure by examining the ones that are left. No questions are allowed, but if the task proves too difficult the child can rearrange the figures in any way he desires. Should the task still be beyond him then more practice is needed in classifying according to size, colour and shape. This could be followed by questions involving just two variables, such as, 'Give me a large red figure?' and then, 'Are there any other large red ones?'

51

Materials. Hoops or circles drawn in chalk on the floor.

Experiences to be gained. Number bonds.

The hoops are placed in a circle and different numerals written i each. These will vary in number according to the ability of the chil dren. Let us suppose 1 to 10 are used. One child stands in the centr of the circle and a number is called out that can be made up by addin two of the numerals in the hoop.

If 9 is used the child may hop into 8 and then into 1 and a seconc child then chooses another combination of two different numbers, say, 6 and 3. This continues until neither player can think of a different combination.

The children score one point for each correct pair provided they can hop into the two hoops. The game can continue with different starting numbers and points could also be given for combinations involving more than two numbers.

If 8 and 1 are used, as above, then 1 and 8 are not acceptable, as the second child should copy the ones used by the first child and merely reverse them.

More than two numbers could be permitted if desired and subtraction of a number could be denoted by raising both hands when hopping into the hoop.

52

Materials. Cuisenaire rods.

Experiences to be gained. Pre-binary arithmetic; number combinations.

Each child is given a white, red, pink and brown rod. The object is to use only these four rods to make, in turn, equivalent lengths to the other six rods. This can then be extended to making greater lengths up to and including the total length of the four original rods.

The parallel cases should also be considered using:

(a) weights of 1, 2, 4 and 8 units

(b) numbers 1, 2, 4 and 8.

In case (a) it will be found that an object weighing any number of units up to, and including 15 can be weighed, and in (b) by using only addition any number up to, and including, 15 can be constructed, e.g. $11 = 8+2+1$, $13 = 8+4+1$.

53

Materials. None.

Experiences to be gained. Angles; counting; simple fractions; left and right.

For the younger children only right angles will be used and they will need to discuss the meaning of a quarter turn (a right angle). Half turns and three-quarter turns could also be used and/or expressed in terms of right angles. They will also need to know left and right.

The playground or the gymnasium will provide the best place to play, but if this is inconvenient as large an area as possible should be cleared in the classroom.

The children form pairs and the game is now illustrated by considering the first pair only. The others follow in turn in a similar way to that now described.

One child is blindfolded and a chalk mark is made on the ground some distance from the child. The partner then gives instructions as to how to reach the mark; these must only contain:
(a) the number of turns or right angles to be made, (b) whether the turn is to the left or right, and (c) the number of paces to be taken.

For example:

'Turn to the right through one right angle. Walk three paces.'
When this has been done the next instructions might be, 'Turn to the left through one right angle. Walk four paces.'

If it is agreed that all turns are to be to the left then a turn through three right angles would replace a turn to the right of one right angle. The older children need not be confined to right angles, but could use any number of degrees in their instructions.

The winning pair is decided by the time taken before one of them is standing within one pace of the chalkmark, or else by the number of instructions that are given.

54

Materials. None.

Experiences to be gained. Spatial visualization and calculation; addition; subtraction.

This game is for two players. Dots are arranged to form a square or rectangular grid as shown. Graph paper could be used and the intersections clearly marked.

Each player makes a line in turn. The lines must join two adjacent dots only and must be horizontal or vertical, not along a diagonal of the small squares formed.

If a player completes a square he places his initials in it and then has an extra turn. This is repeated for every square completed so that a player may be able to complete several squares at one turn.

When the game is completed each player adds up the number of squares with his initials in it. These totals are subtracted to give the player with the larger number his score for that game.

55

Materials. Chalk or cards.

Experiences to be gained. Addition; subtraction; number bonds.

A large circle is drawn on the floor and numerals are written around it or else on cards that are placed at equal intervals on the circumference.

If practice is needed in bonds involving a certain number, say 9, then a child stands at the centre of the circle with his eyes shut and is turned around several times. He then opens his eyes and states the number he is facing (or the nearest one if there is not one directly in front of him). He then gives the sum of the number and 9.

Practice in the subtraction of numbers from one to ten can be done by limiting the numerals around the circle to those greater than ten, unless of course negative numbers are required. Alternatively, they could always subtract the smaller number from the greater, but this artificial procedure is not to be recommended as it often leads to the impression that, for instance, 3 – 9 is the same 9 – 3.

56

Materials. Graph paper; two counters.

Experiences to be gained. Spatial ideas.

This game is for two players. Each has a counter and the game will be illustrated by playing on a board as shown below.

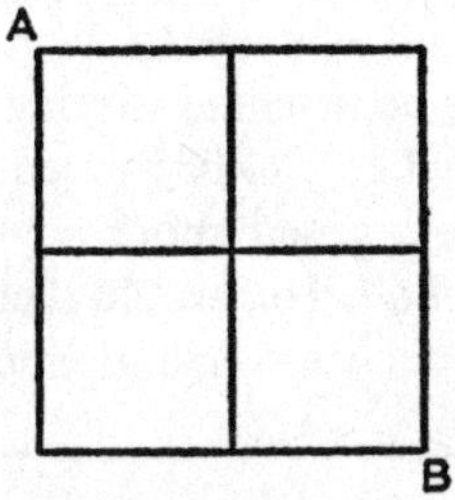

The game is often called Cops and Robbers. The cop starts at A and the robber at B, the cop having the first move. Each move is along one side of a small square. The children should be left to reach their own conclusions about this case and then they should play the game with the robber moving first.

After these two simple cases the game should be extended to a network with more squares and also to irregular shapes. For example:

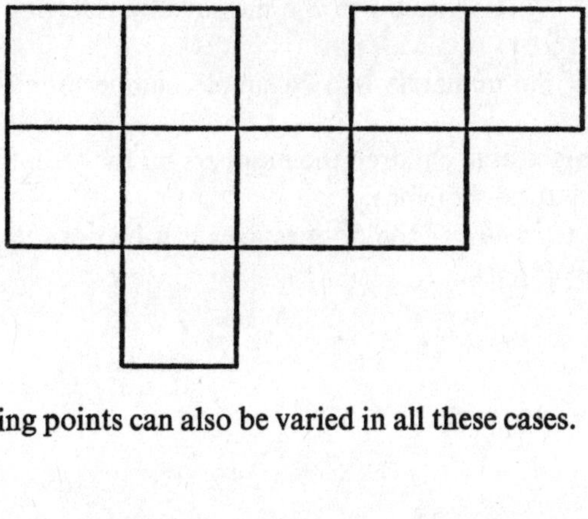

The starting points can also be varied in all these cases.

57

Materials. Seven matches.

Experiences to be gained. Shapes and their properties.

Using all seven matches the children make a triangle. They then attempt to make different triangles, again using all the seven matches each time. (Only two such triangles are possible, one with 3, 3 and 1 and the other with 2, 2 and 3 matches.)

Similar problems can be invented varying the number of matches and also the shape of the figure to be formed.

In the original problem posed above any number of the matches could be used, instead of all. This would then include triangles made with 1, 1, 1 and 2, 2, 1 matches, to mention just two.

58

Materials. A strip with the letters of the alphabet on it, each with a numeral 1 to 26 under it.

Experiences to be gained. Counting; recognition of numerals.

One child decides on a simple message and taps or knocks the corresponding number of times for each letter needed. Other children count silently and hence write down the message by referring to the strip mentioned above.

Instead of the numerals 1 to 26 simple number bonds or pictures could be used.

For the more able children the numbers on the strip can be varied from their natural sequence.

Many other ways of coding messages can be used to give further experiences of this kind.

59

Materials. Graph paper or card.

Experiences to be gained. Area; perimeter; shapes; rotation; reflection.

Each child has three squares cut from the graph paper. These have to be arranged in as many ways as possible; any sides that touch must do so completely. The different shapes can be stuck onto card.

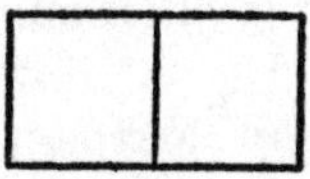

Correct

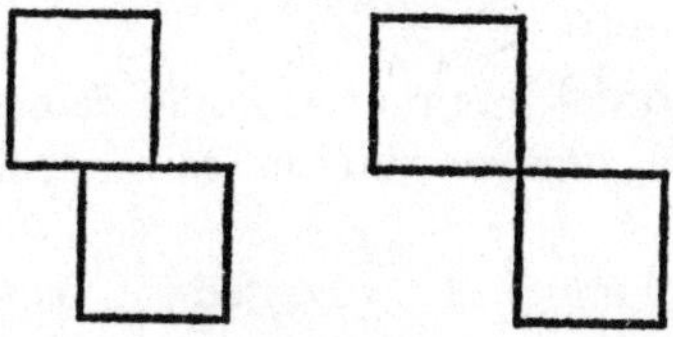

Not correct

Reflections and rotations do not count as separate cases, for instance the following two shapes are really the same and could be obtained by either operation.

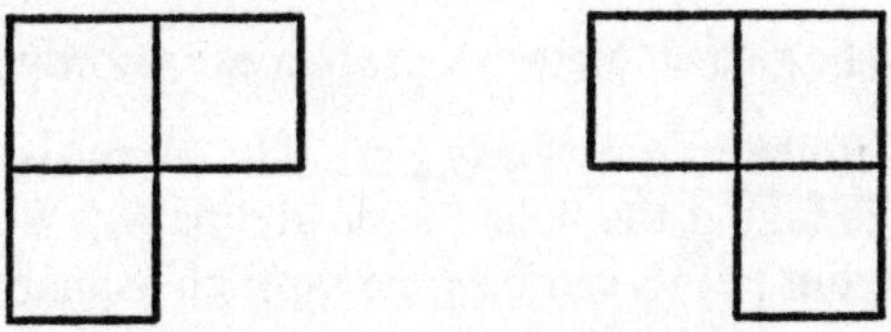

Four squares can be dealt with in a similar way.

Some children may care to use bricks to investigate the problem in three dimensions.

60

Materials. Ten cards, each with one numeral on it (1 to 10).

Experiences to be gained. Order of the numerals; recording.

The first of two players places the cards in a line so that the numerals are in order, 1 to 10. Two of the cards have their positions interchanged, then another two and so on, until the cards are thoroughly mixed. The second player can interchange any two of the cards at a time, the object being to rearrange the order of the cards so that they read 1 to 10.

The order when mixed could be noted and several children could then play and see who can rearrange them in the smallest number of moves.

The number of cards used can be varied to suit the ability of the children, very young ones starting with only the numbers 1, 2 and 3.

61

Materials. None.

Experiences to be gained. Network properties; recording.

Any number of children can take part. The object is to draw given figures without taking the pencil from the paper. No line must be covered twice, but points can be gone through as many times as one likes. There is complete freedom regarding the choice of a starting point.

Even the youngest children will have no difficulty with (a) but may experience some with (b).

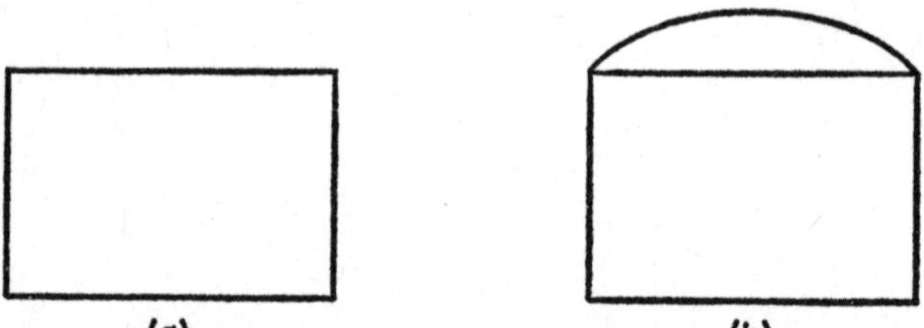

(a) (b)

Children should be encouraged to draw their own figures and exchange them. This not only ensures that they are working on their own problems as opposed to those of the teacher, but also encourages creativity. The need to record the solution, after constructing a problem, will become apparent when other children fail to solve it, and challenge whether there really is a solution.

Many figures will have no solution, for example (c) or (d) which can be seen to be equivalent.

(c)

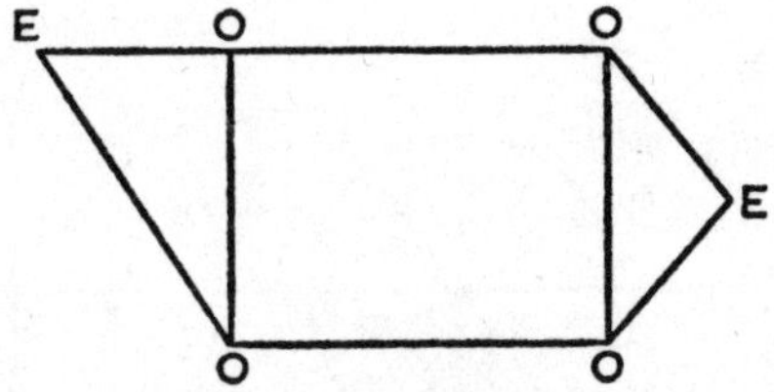

(d)

The lines or intersections could be numbered in succession so as to facilitate recording. This can be further aided by the use of arrows and crayons. These matters are best left to the children as many will not be ready for this stage. (Note: If an odd number of lines meet at a point denote it by O, and for an even number write E. See (d) above. If more than two points are marked O the network cannot be traced without taking the pencil from the paper. Why? Why is it really unnecessary to mark the two points E in (d)?)

62

Materials. Mirrors without a frame.

Experiences to be gained. Symmetry and reflection.

Simple figures with lines of symmetry (square, circle) are provided and the children place mirrors so that the reflection completes the figure. The dotted lines show some of the possible positions for the mirror. The children can find other examples and draw them.

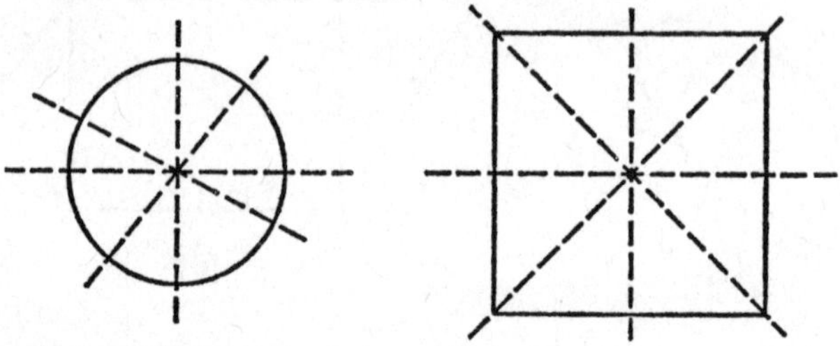

Half a figure is next provided and with the aid of the mirror the complete figure can be drawn.

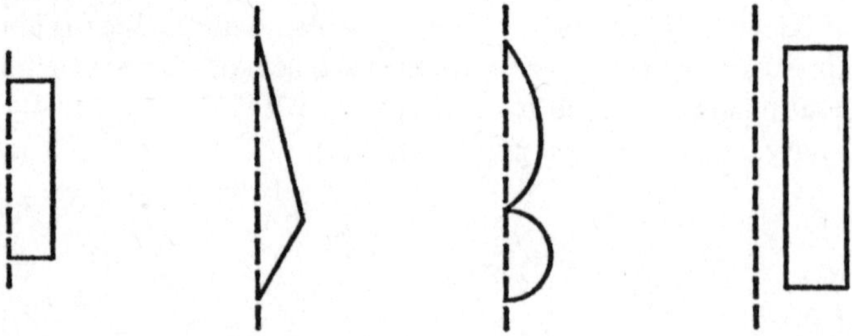

The children should then try to complete half figures, without the aid of the mirror. This can however be used by them to check their answers.

63

Materials. Graph paper or a number line; squares cut from card (2 cm is a convenient length for the sides).

Experiences to be gained. Even numbers; counting in twos.

Strips of graph paper, preferably the same width as the cards, are arranged in a line. The length will depend on how many even numbers are to be considered; with cards of sides 2 cm and even numbers up to 20 a length of 20 cm would be required.

The game is best played by two children. The cards are thoroughly mixed and then placed face downwards in a pile.

The players take a card in turn and place it in its correct position on the line, i.e. so that when completed the numerals will be in the order 2, 4, 6, 8, 10, 12 . . . . etc.

Incorrectly placed cards can be placed to one side of their correct position. For example, suppose the first player has correctly placed 6 and 10 and the second player places 4 correctly but puts 14 in the wrong position; the cards would then be arranged as indicated below.

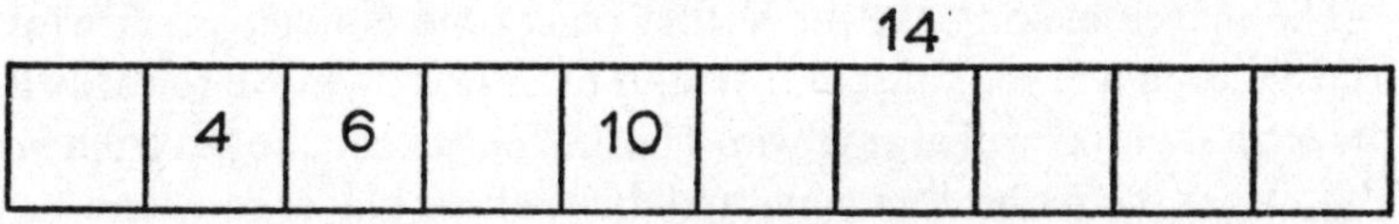

Note that the card marked 14 has been moved from its incorrect position to one outside its correct place. If one player's wrong cards are placed on one side of the line and his opponent's on the opposite side the winner can easily be determined by seeing who makes the least errors.

As an alternative the wrongly placed cards could be replaced at the bottom of the pile of cards. Scoring could also be done by the players placing their cards on different sides of the line. This has the additional advantage of requiring only a single line to play on. The line would be marked at intervals spaced at lengths equal to the side of cards used.

Even numbers, multiples of three and many other adaptations can be used, these being of the greatest value if they are suggested by the children.

64

Materials. Graph paper; a counter.

Experiences to be gained. Calculations; imagery; odd and even.

This game is for two players. A board such as that shown below is marked on, or cut out of, graph paper. The counter is placed at A and each player takes it in turn to move it, a move being along the side of a square.

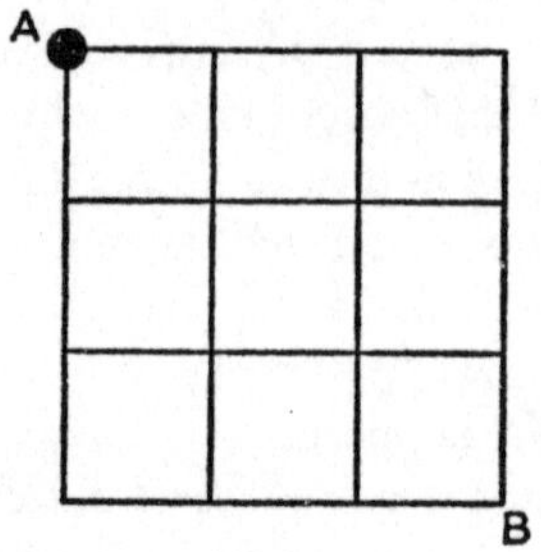

The player making the move that places the counter on B wins. The children will soon discover that, if both players move towards B, the second player will always win. The first player can, however, move away from B after his first move and then neither player can win.

This should lead to suggestions by the children for changes in the rules, e.g. no move is to take the counter farther away from B.

What happens if other starting points are used instead of A?

What happens if each player has two moves at a time?

Starting at any one point the number of moves needed to reach B could be noted and a relationship with odd or even established for each point.

65

Materials. Cuisenaire rods.

Experiences to be gained. Simple fractions; equivalence; odd and even.

Two small rods, e.g. red, are placed end to end, and a child is asked to find one rod which is of the same length (pink). The idea of simple fractions consisting of parts that are equal can be discussed and other rods illustrating 'a half' found.

Replacing the two equal rods by one of equivalent length can be extended to larger chains, for example two blue rods are the same length as one orange and one brown rod. Reversing the procedure is more difficult as a child then needs to find two rods of equal length that will be equivalent to a given rod. Rods that are an odd number of centimetres in length (e.g. blue), cannot be partitioned into two equal lengths by using the rods, and consequently the concept of odd and even is experienced in a preliminary form.

By using three equal rods we can introduce one-third, two-thirds and similarly other fractions.

It is important to stress that there are many ways of representing any one fraction with the rods, and the children should be encouraged to answer questions in a variety of ways and not just give one answer. There are, for instance, many ways of representing one-third and not just by using a white (w) and a light green (lg) rod. (2w, 2lg), (3w, 3lg), (r, dg), (2r, 2dg), (lg, B) are just a few.

dg dark green; B blue.

66

Materials. Cuisenaire rods.

Experiences to be gained. Equivalence of lengths.

The game is for two or three players. One acts as banker and gives the others some rods, for instance two orange rods. The banker is asked, by specific questioning to exchange rods for rods equivalent in length. For example, 'Give me a blue and a white rod for this orange one.'

The player asking for rods scores a point if his request is correct, the banker and any other players having the right to challenge his statement.

This can also be played with strips of cards representing different lengths if the rods are not available.

67

Materials. Graph paper.

Experiences to be gained. Spatial appreciation; area; counting.

Three squares each containing sixteen smaller squares are cut out of graph paper. One of the three squares is used as the 'board' on which the game will be played and the other two squares are cut into two sets of shapes. These sets will contain pieces of the same shape and one possible set is shown below. The sizes and shapes can be varied according to the wishes of the players.

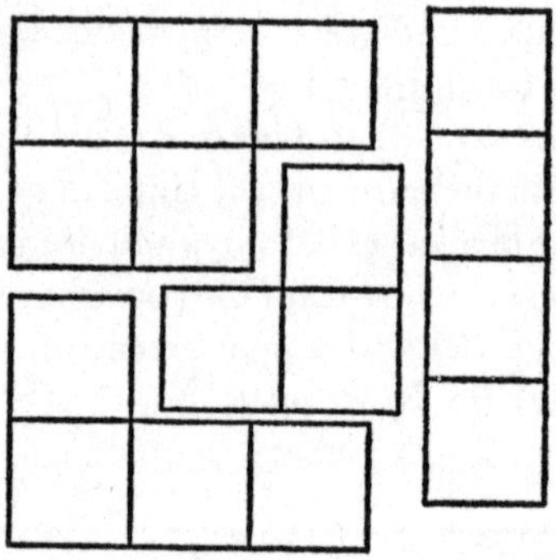

Two players each have one set of the shapes described and play commences with one of them placing a shape on the 'board' so that the small squares on the shape coincide with those on the 'board'. The second player now places one of his pieces and the children then play alternately until neither can place any more. The small squares on the pieces not played are now totalled by each player, the one with the smaller number being the winner. When playing subsequent games, the players should 'take turns' at having the first move.

Children could also try to find as many ways as possible to fit one set of shapes on to the 'board'. This would lead to solutions that are symmetrical and ones produced by rotation. A need to record the results would naturally arise so as to ensure that solutions were not repeated.

68

Materials. Graph paper; two counters of one colour and two of another colour.

Experiences to be gained. Mental imagery; symmetry.

This game is for two players (A and B). A strip of graph paper is cut out as shown. The length can be varied. The counters are placed at the

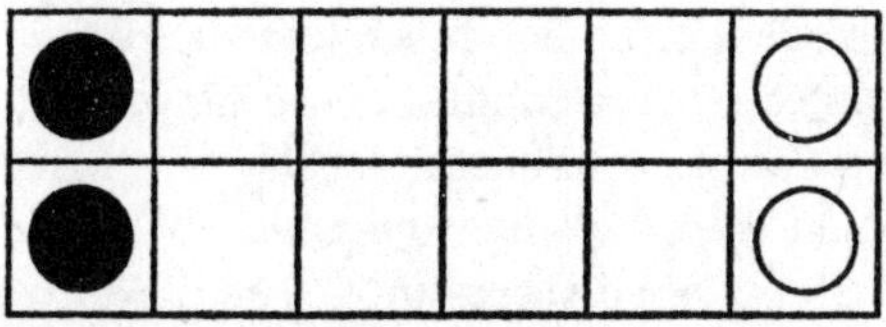

ends (see diagram) and we will assume A has the two on the left (black) and B has the two on the right (white).

The object is to block the opponents counters so that they cannot be moved. A counter can be moved any number of squares at a time, but only in one direction, black to the right and white to the left. With correct play the second person to move should always win. Why? A feel for symmetry will help and this is why it is included under 'Experiences'. Do not, however, look for a direct application but rather one such as Alice might have seen in the Looking Glass.

69

Materials. None.

Experiences to be gained. Number bonds.

Any number of children can play. One should act as leader and he will state a number, say eight. Each player takes it in turn to express eight in the form of an addition bond and this continues until no more bonds are suggested. If after $7 + 1$, $3 + 5$, $8 + 0$ and $5 + 3$ the next player cannot suggest a bond then he scores 0 for that particular turn and the other players continue. The player failing to answer should not drop out of the game but has his turn on the next round. The leader should record all the suggestions and give one point to each player naming a bond successfully. The player with the highest score at the end is the winner.

A systematic follow-up by the group would ensure that all the addition bonds are covered. If subtraction is allowed then there are an infinite number of bonds, $9 - 1$, $10 - 2$, $11 - 3$, $12 - 4$ and so on. For the older children multiplication and division could be used and even a combination of these for the very able, e.g. $(8 \div 2) + (2 \times 2)$. Such work is more suited to a written game with a generous time allowance.

70

Materials. Four pink rods; three light green rods (Cuisenaire).

Experiences to be gained. Combinations of rectangles.

The problem is to make a square using all seven of the rods.

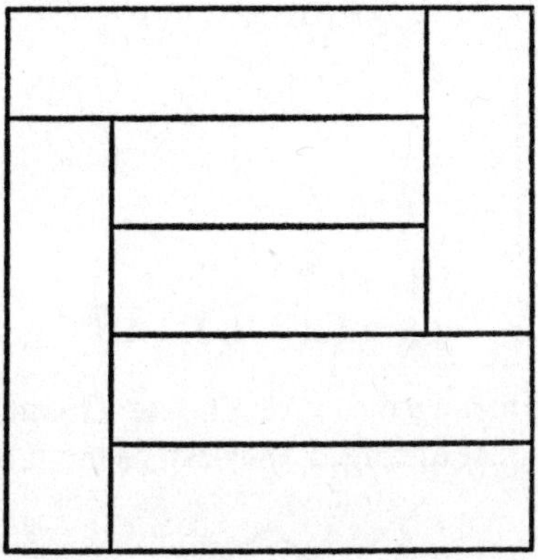

One solution is shown above. Others obtained by the children should be examined to see whether they can be obtained from the one above by rotation or reflection.

By first making up a square with other combinations of rods, children can construct their own problems. Before disarranging the rods the original square should be recorded by drawing; this will enable other children to check their solutions against that of the child composing the problem.

71

Materials. Shapes cut out of paper or card.

Experiences to be gained. Creative work with shapes.

A limited number of shapes are given to each child and they arrange these to represent various objects. For example:

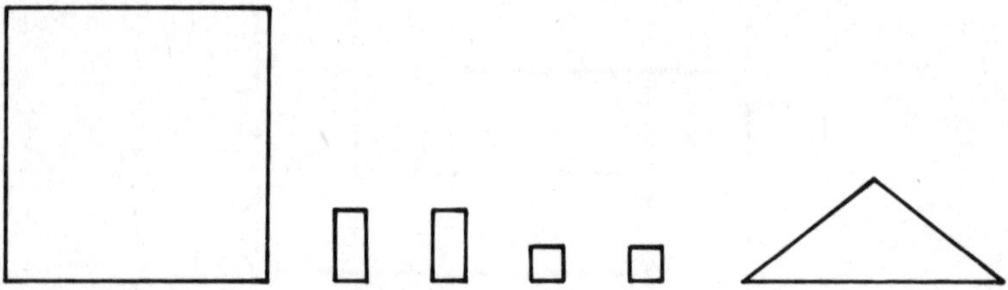

These might be arranged to give a house. Gummed paper is to be preferred so that, once arranged, they can be mounted.

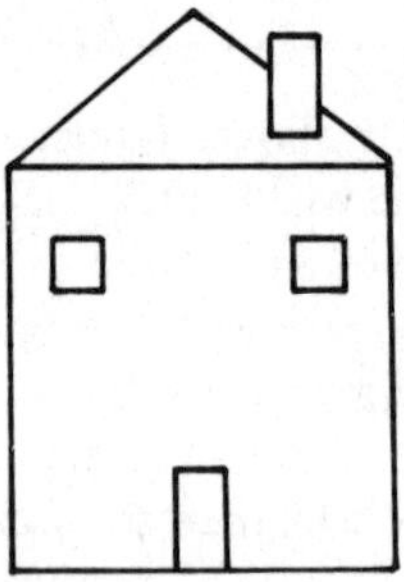

The procedure could be reversed by the children drawing a figure containing squares, rectangles, triangles and circles. They then cut out the required shapes to cover their figure and present these to other children to rearrange.

Written work should be encouraged. In the above example this might consist of, 'I used a large square, two small squares, two small rectangles and a large triangle to make a house.'

Harder puzzles involving tangrams provide a useful extension of this work.

72

Materials. None.

Experiences to be gained. Shapes.

Each group of children chooses a shape—triangle, rectangle, square, circle or any other that is within their experience. In a given time, they make a list of all examples of this shape that they can find.

A mere five minutes has produced some excellent results, but a project lasting a week could also be successfully used.

In both cases books could be made, such as 'Our Book of Squares'. Follow-up is essential if the maximum value is to be gained from such activities.

The children could be taken on a 'Shape Walk', the localities being as varied as possible—shops, park, school and so on. Holiday time and school trips will enrich the work, but home and television can provide many examples.

The shapes need not be confined to two dimensions as cylinders, cubes, cuboids and other three-dimensional objects come naturally before the two-dimensional cases.

The idea of a 'Walk' can be used for other mathematical concepts besides 'Shape'. Consider the possibilities in a 'Number Walk'.

73

Materials. Stop-watch or watch with a seconds hand.

Experiences to be gained. Use of watch; time; recording.

An activity such as reading one page, running a certain distance or doing a jig-saw is selected by the children. The time taken for each child to do the task is recorded and could be represented graphically.

The children should be encouraged to make estimates whenever possible and compare these with the actual time taken. This personal involvement is a major factor in developing a sense of time and the ability to estimate and compare periods.

This work can be followed by asking the children to estimate various periods of time that are longer and more difficult, such as might be experienced when reading a book or going for a long walk.

Occupied and unoccupied time can be illustrated by asking children to estimate thirty seconds when

(a) they are doing nothing;
(b) they are occupied (drawing, reading, etc.).

If these times are recorded it will be found that (b) is nearly always far longer than (a).

74

Materials. Ten counters, five of one colour and five of another.

Experiences to be gained. Simple counting; mental imagery and spatial calculations.

The two players have five counters each, each set being all of the same colour. A Noughts and Crosses board is drawn. The players take it in turn to place a counter, the object being to get three counters in a row.

After some experience of the game the children can be asked questions such as:

(a) Why are ten counters used? Could it be played with only nine?

(b) If there is good play on both sides decide whether
    (i) the first player should win
    (ii) the second player should win
    (iii) the game should be a draw.

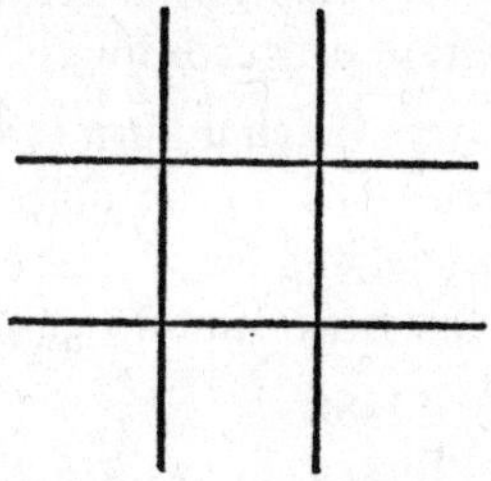

The children should also be asked to consider the possibility that, even with good play, the result can vary from game to game.

An interesting variation occurs when the first player to get three counters in a line loses.

The standard game can be extended by drawing in two extra lines, the winner then being the first player to get four counters in a line.

75

Materials. About thirty beads, conkers, shells or other suitable counting material.

Experiences to be gained. Addition; subtraction; combining and anticipating these operations; recording.

The game is for two players. Each in turn can take one, two or three objects. The last player to pick up an object wins. The number of objects can be varied in each game if desired. Suppose the players (A and B) start with twelve beads and the game proceeds as follows:

A takes 3,	B takes 1.	(8 remain)
A takes 2,	B takes 3.	(3 remain)
A takes 2,	B takes 1.	

B picked up the last bead and therefore won. A played very badly as he could have picked up three beads on the last turn and hence won.

The children should be encouraged to see how early they can forecast the winner. If there are four beads left the person to play next is in a losing position; once this is appreciated the older children may be able to foresee the previous stage—for example if there are six beads the one to play announces he will win by taking two beads and leaving his opponent with the losing position, i.e. four beads.

Very young children have the experience of counting 1, 2 and 3 beads, and a practical example of subtraction, but they may not appreciate the strategies described above.

Recording and subsequent discussion and analysis of the strategies involved will only be of value if they are carefully gauged to suit the ability of the children.

76

Materials. Card.

Experiences to be gained. Addition; subtraction; inequalities and a variety of other experiences.

Each child writes a number on a card and these are then placed in line.

For example this might result in

3, 8, 5, 14, 19, 1, 11, 43.

The children take it in turn to make up a number sentence or story, about successive pairs, such as:

3 is less than 8

5 needed 9 more added to it to make 14

19 people were in a bus and one more got in. There were then 20 people in the bus.

There were 11 boys in a class of 43 children; this means there were 32 girls.

Note that in general a third number will be involved, but this is not essential as can be seen by the first example. If the third number had been asked for the answer might have been

'3 is less than 8. It is 5 less.'

77

Materials. None.

Experiences to be gained. Addition; number patterns.

Two children each choose a number less than ten. They then take it in turns to write down their numbers and add up all the numbers written so far. The first to reach 100 or more wins. Suppose one chooses 8 and the other 7 the totals would read 8, 15, 23, 30, 38, 45, 53, 60, 68, 75, 83, 90, 98, 105. The player who chose 7 therefore wins as it was his turn that made the total greater than 100.

The children need not of course add the numbers mentally. Number patterns will emerge from such series and are worth discussing. For example

(a) Starting with any one number the next but one to it is found by adding 15 or else by subtracting 15.

(b) The sequence of the units figure is 8, 5, 3, 0. This would continue if the numbers were increased beyond 105.

The target number of 100 in the above example can be modified according to the ability of the children and similarly the numbers which they choose can be varied.

An interesting modification is to allow the children to vary the number they choose each time. The winning strategies for these games are not likely to be of interest until a later age than we are considering, but, as the end of a game approaches, many children will be able to forecast who will be the winner.

For example, in the sequence of the first game given above it is very obvious after 98 who will win and also quite simple for many children once 90 is reached. When observing children playing this game it is instructive to ask them to tell you as soon as they can see who will be the winner.

78

Materials. Card in three different colours.

Experiences to be gained. Classifying by several criteria.

This game is best suited for two, three, four or six players. As in Number 50 a large triangle, circle, square and rectangle are cut in each of the three colours, which we will again suppose to be red, yellow and blue. Similarly small figures are cut out in each shape and colour mentioned, so that there are twenty-four altogether.

The figures are distributed evenly amongst the players and the first player places any one of his figures on the table. Suppose this is a large red circle. The second player can put down any shape that differs in exactly one attribute, i.e. shape, size or colour, but is unchanged in the other attributes.

The large red circle could therefore be followed by any of the following: a small red circle, a large yellow circle, a large blue circle, a large red triangle, a large red square or a large red rectangle. When this second piece has been put on the table the third player (and those after him) will have more choice. The third player must follow with a piece differing in one attribute, but it can differ from that of the first or the second player.

In general as the line of figures becomes longer the players can play pieces differing in one attribute from either of the figures at the end of the line.

Variations can be introduced by making the figures differ in two (or three) attributes. Another popular method follows the main game as described above, but also allows figures differing in two attributes to be placed at right angles to those in the line.

79

Materials. None.

Experiences to be gained. Classifying; intersection.

The children go to opposite ends of the room according to which of two categories they belong.

For example: Boys/Girls.

Those wearing glasses/Those not wearing glasses.

The categories used should include all the children.

After sufficient experience with this work the partitioning can involve more than two categories, e.g. choose which colour you like best out of red, yellow and blue.

More difficult questions arise when some of the children are left out. (Those who come to school in a bus and those who come in a car, thus excluding those that walk to school.)

The next complication to consider is when a child, or any object, comes into two categories. One category could be boys and the other all children wearing glasses. A class of seven-year-olds decided to draw a line across the middle of the room and boys with glasses stood with one foot on one side and one foot on the other.

This concrete work with children can be followed by using toys and other concrete objects; it should gradually be made more abstract and Venn diagrams introduced.

The following is used to illustrate Venn diagrams; it was done by a group of seven-year-old children. They made up the problem and the answers.

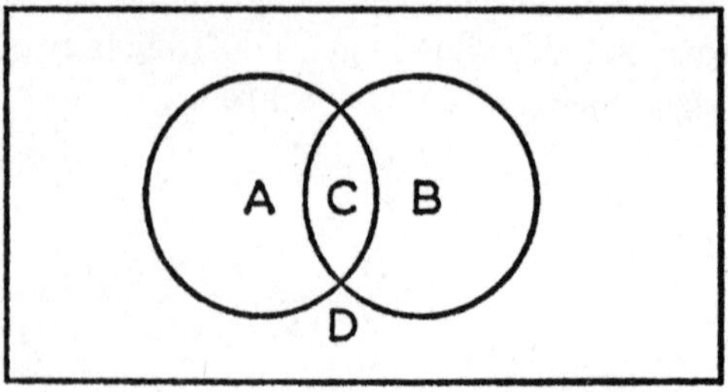

A. Animals that can fly but not swim (flies, eagles). B. Animals that can swim but not fly (fish, frogs). C. Animals that can fly and swim (duck, sea-gull). D. Animals that cannot fly or swim (teacher, cats).

The shapes used should be varied and not always be circles.

The figure shown was a rectangle of sides about one metre and 50 cm. Some children cut out pictures of animals, others drew them; the names of the animals were added. The pictures were then stuck on to the figure. Many arguments arose about the definitions of animal, insect, etc., and this gave rise to useful follow-up lessons.

The children should suggest as many of the classifications as possible, rather than the teacher doing most of the constructive work.

80

Materials. Graph paper; counters; mirror.

Experiences to be gained. Elementary co-ordinate ideas; 1–1 correspondence; symmetry and reflection.

A rectangle is cut out of graph paper and the lines emphasized. A child places counters of various colours in the squares and is then given another rectangle that has the same dimensions as the original one. The object is to place counters exactly as those on the first rectangle.

If successful at this a mirror can be placed so as to enable the child to see the image of the rectangle and counters.

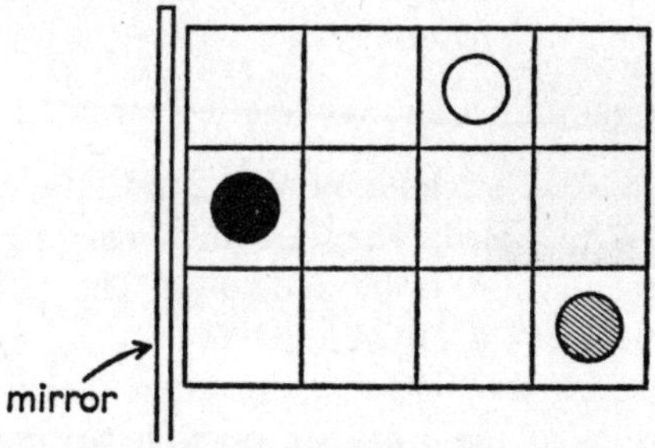

The second rectangle is now placed on the left of the mirror and the child asked to place counters on it as they appear in the mirror image. If they are successful, similar problems can be set without using the mirror.

Instead of using counters marks could be made, or figures drawn, in the squares. These could then be coloured.

81

Materials. Blackboard and chalk.

Experiences to be gained. Vocabulary.

Some words are written on the blackboard, such as 'large', 'larger', 'tall', 'fat'. The teacher may have chosen these so as to give experience in their use or to find which children are using them incorrectly.

The children can be asked to write a short story, using all the given words. The following is an example by an eight-year-old girl.

> There was a tall man and he was going shopping with his wife who was very fat.
> That is a nice coat said the wife. I think I will buy it.
> You will need a very large size said the man and they went into the shop.
> She tried on the coat but it was too small. Have you got a larger one she asked the shop lady.
> Yes, she said and she buyed it.

82

Materials. Any three different objects.

Experiences to be gained. Order; systematic approach; recording.

The objects which we will denote by A, B and C, are placed in a line and their order is recorded. They are then rearranged to give a different order, then a third order and so on. The results might, for three arrangements, be ABC, BCA and CBA.

The children are asked to find as many different orders as they can. In the case considered there are six possible arrangements ABC, ACB, BAC, BCA, CAB and CBA. The children who are successful could extend this game to four objects A, B, C and D. There are then twenty-four different orders.

The teacher should discuss the method used in solving the last problem, so as to discover whether a systematic approach was used. If not then tasks such as writing down all the arrangements where A is on the left, followed by similar lists for B, C and D should help.

The children should notice there are the same numbers in each of the four lists and, by suitable questions, they can be led to see that each of these three lists has a connection with the arrangements of three objects as found earlier.

The younger and less able children will need a more concrete approach. They should use separate sets of objects each time, for example six red, six yellow and six blue counters would enable them to make the six possible arrangements of three objects. The method of recording and using only three objects could follow later.

83

Materials. A cardboard box; balls (or building bricks).

Experiences to be gained. Counting; number bonds; recording.

A child throws a given number of balls, say eight, trying to get them into a box. The distance must be adjusted according to the throwing skill of the child. The number in the box, and also those that fall outside, are counted and recorded.

A second child then does the same so that the score after three games might be as follows:

	John			*Mary*		
IN	3	4	1	2	5	6
OUT	5	4	7	6	3	2

'John got eight in the box and Mary got 13 in. Mary won by 5.'

The children should be encouraged to discover the facts such as the sum of the IN and OUT columns always being 8, the total of 24 for all the numbers involving John, and similarly for Mary.

The ideas involved can be extended to more games in which blank spaces are left in the table so that another child has to calculate the missing numbers. By varying the number of balls used other number bonds can be practised.

84

Materials. Card.

Experiences to be gained. Counting; spatial arrangements.

Twelve trees or plants are cut out with a base that can be bent over for them to stand on.

Bend along dotted line.

Arrange the trees so that there are three lines with four trees in each line.

Now use only ten of the trees and place them so that there are still four in each line.

The children should make up similar problems, recording their solutions, and then exchange the problems.

85

Materials. Discs or bottle tops or cards; three bags.

Experiences to be gained. Number bonds; recording.

Two of the bags contain discs with numerals painted or stuck on them. The third bag of discs is placed between the other two and contains only signs $>$, $<$, $+$, $-$, $\times$, $\div$, $=$, or else written instructions (add, subtract, etc.).

These will all be varied to suit the ability of the children.

A child takes one disc from each bag and places them on the table with the sign between the numerals. This can be recorded if required.

Where applicable (e.g. $5 + 3$) the child states, and perhaps records, the answer. In cases such as $3 > 5$ he states whether the sentence is TRUE or NOT TRUE.

$>$ means is greater than.

$<$ means is less than.

86

Materials. Toy cars or counters; a die; graph paper.

Experiences to be gained. Counting; addition; subtraction; recording.

Any number of children can play; each is provided with a car (or a counter). A race-track for five players could be marked out as shown, but many other variations are possible.

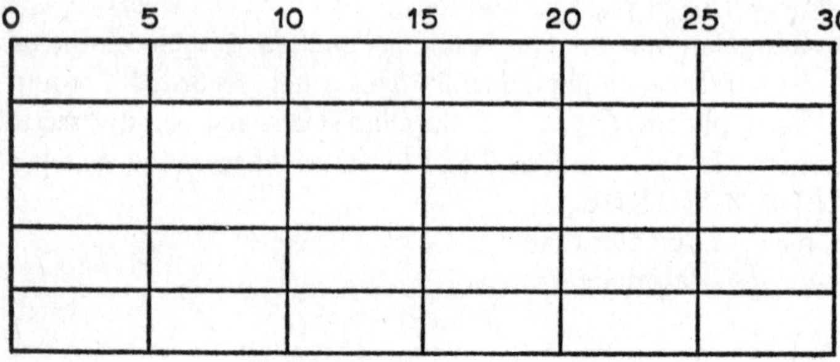

Each player throws the die in turn and records his score. When he has five or more he can move his car from the starting position up to the line marked 5. If he scored 6 he would only move the car to the 5 line but would count the remaining 1 towards his next score.

Suppose a player throws successively 3, 4, 6, 2, 1 and 5. The manner in which he records and calculates should be left to him and guidance given only if requested. A common form is as follows:

3	3
+4 (He moves his car to the	+2 (He moves his car to the
7 5 line)	5 15 line)
−5	−5
2	0
+6 He moves his car to the	+1
8 10 line)	1
−5	+5 (He moves his car to the
3	6 20 line)

In the case illustrated the first player to reach 30 is the winner and the total scores can then be checked by addition.

For young children all the numerals could be written in. Larger or smaller numbers than thirty could be used and multiples of numbers other than five would also suffice.

87

Materials. Card.

Experiences to be gained. Area; counting; filling space.

This game is for two players. About thirty squares (2 cm is a convenient length for the sides) are cut out of card. A rectangular sheet is also cut out so that the squares will just fit on it if arranged in rows.

(Each square is 4 cm^2 in area, therefore the 30 squares occupy 120 cm^2. The rectangle could therefore have sides 12 cm and 10 cm or 8 cm and 15 cm.)

Each player in turn places a square anywhere on the card and the last one to put down a square is the winner.

The squares must not overlap, and those already played cannot be moved.

At first children tend to place the squares in rows and this has its value. An appreciation of odd and even as well as addition and multiplication can arise. The main problem, however, is when the squares are placed in an irregular way.

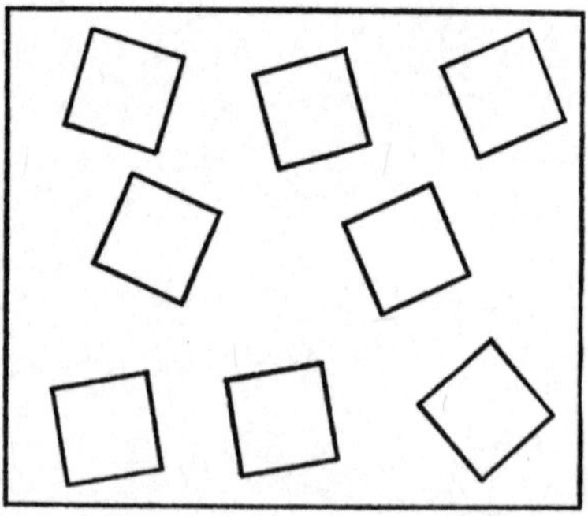

The children should be encouraged, as the game nears its end, to forecast who will win.

88

Material. None.

Experiences to be gained. Simple multiples or division.

This game is for older children as they need to appreciate which numbers are divisible by three, i.e. exact multiples of three. The children count in turn but instead of saying three (or any multiple of three) they say 'BUZZ'. The sequence will thus be—one, two, buzz, four, five, buzz, seven, eight, buzz and so on. Even children who cannot state the numbers that are multiples of three can often say 'BUZZ' in the correct place due to the rhythm of the sequence.

If a child gives the wrong answer, or hesitates unduly, they drop out and the others continue until only one remains.

It is convenient to have all the children standing at the start and they can then sit down when they drop out. The teacher can more easily point to each child whose turn it is if this routine is adopted.

When only a few children remain the game can be made more difficult by also including all numbers containing a three—13, 30, 31 and so on.

A number game, 'WHIZZ', involves seven and its multiples and 'WHIZZ-BUZZ' would combine both seven and three. This will prove too difficult for all but the oldest and most able, the sequence now being one, two, buzz, four, five, buzz, whizz, eight, buzz, ten,
1 2 3 4 5 6 7 8 9 10
eleven, buzz, buzz, whizz, buzz, sixteen and so on.
11 12 13 14 15 16

89

Materials. Three dice or children's building bricks.

Experiences to be gained. Addition; subtraction; multiplication; division; recording.

Three dice can be used, one with $+$, $-$, $\div$, $\times$ on it and the others numbered 1, 2, 3, 4, 5, 6. Both types are available commercially but building bricks are quite satisfactory with the symbols written on them in chalk, or, for greater permanency, paper can be stuck to the faces and the symbols written on the paper.

According to the age and ability of the children the symbols used can be limited. For example some 6-year-olds might have the numbers 1,1,2,3,4,5 on two dice and $+$ and $-$ on three faces each of the third die.

Each child throws the three dice together or turns them out of the box if they are too large to handle. He then writes down the larger number, then the sign $+$, $-$, $\div$, or $\times$ and finally the smaller number. The resulting number is calculated and recorded, the winner is the one whose score is the larger.

For the older and more able children several scores can be totalled before the winner is decided but since fractions may be involved one turn each is enough for many children. In this case they can play a series of, say, nine games.

If the order is not fixed as stated, but varied, then negative numbers can be used. Should this be desired the numbered dice could be of different colours and the order fixed by an agreed order of colours.

90

Materials. None.

Experiences to be gained. Spatial visualization and calculation. Adding simple fractions.

A lattice arrangement of dots is drawn as shown or the intersections of lines on graph paper can be used.

Starting at any dot, and without taking the pencil from the paper, squares are drawn connecting the given dots. Only horizontal and vertical lines are permitted. It is forbidden to go over a line already drawn.

The object is to complete as many squares as possible. One point is scored for every such square, three-quarters of a point if three sides only are completed, half a point for two sides and one point for one side. This game could be played on a geo-board using thread or shirring elastic.

91

Materials. Six counters, three of one colour and three of another.

Experiences to be gained. Mental imagery and spatial calculations.

A square is drawn on paper and divided into four sections as shown.

For convenience in explaining the game the points where lines intersect have been numbered.

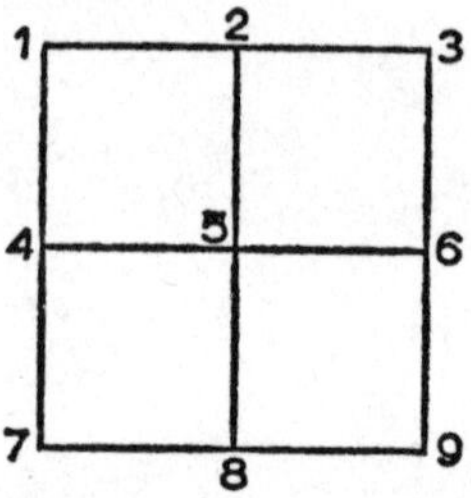

Two players are required and the object is to get three counters in a line. As in noughts and crosses this could be along a diagonal so 1, 5, 9 and 3, 5, 7 are winning arrangements.

The six counters are played and it is unlikely that this will result in a win for either player. To illustrate the rest of the play we will assume the counters are in the following position and that it is white's turn to move.

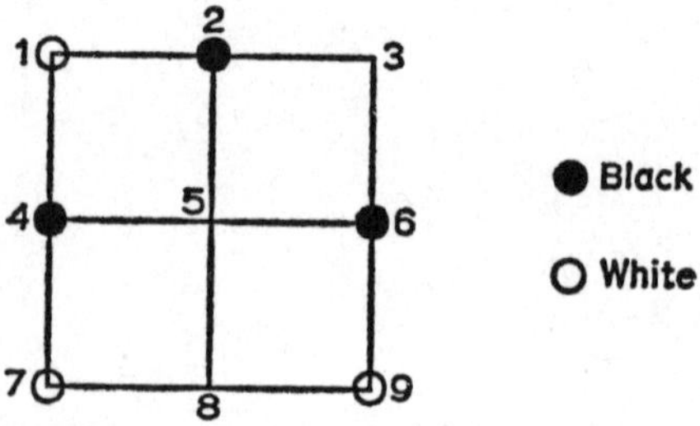

White can move any one of his counters but it can move along one of the drawn lines and can only go to a place that is not occupied already. A counter cannot jump over another one so the only possible moves are with the counters at 7 and 9. Either of them can be moved to 8. Black will then move his counter from 2 to 5 and hence win.

92

Materials. Graph paper; counters in two different colours.

Experiences to be gained. Mental imagery; pattern and rhythm in space and movement.

This game is for one player. A strip of graph paper is cut out and four counters (black and white) placed on it as shown below. The object

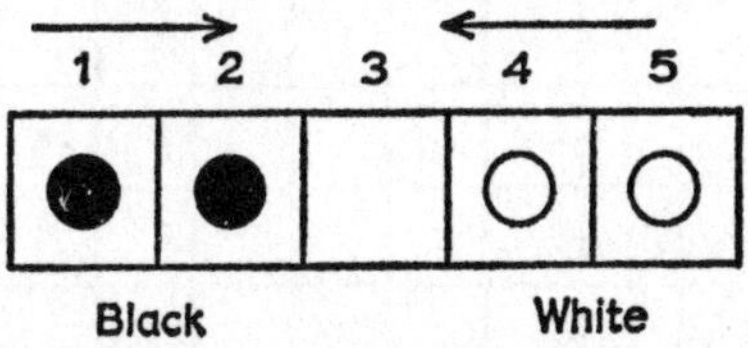

is to exchange the position of the counters so that the black ones are on the right and the white ones on the left.

A move consists of moving a counter one space in the direction shown (see diagram) or in jumping over a counter (of either colour) in the next square provided the square on the other side is vacant.

For example, in the diagram the counter in 5 could jump to 3; the counter in 1 could jump to 3; the counter in 2 could move to 3 or the one in 4 could move to 3.

The game can be extended by using more counters and children find it of considerable interest to see who can exchange the counters in the least number of moves. This leads to an interest in recording the result as the children often fail when asked to repeat the solution.

93

Materials. Graph paper.

Experiences to be gained. Co-ordinates.

Two axes are drawn on graph paper and labelled as shown. The game is for two players each of which will have a piece of graph paper as described.

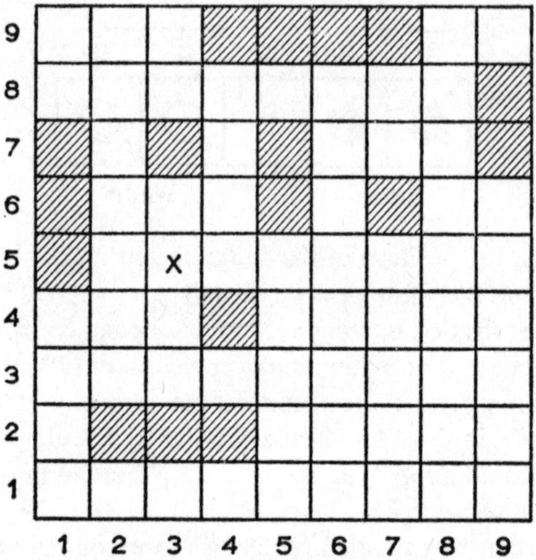

Each player shades in squares to represent the ships in two opposing fleets. These can be placed anywhere on the diagram but the opponent must not be allowed to see where they are placed.

The fleets each consist of

three submarines each occupying one square;
two destroyers each occupying two squares;
two cruisers each occupying three squares;
one battleship occupying four squares

The players take it in turn to fire a torpedo by guessing the position of a square. 3, 5 means the 3rd column and the 5th row and hence hits the square marked X. Practice in this notation can be given as a preliminary exercise and particular care should be taken to ensure the players do not confuse 3, 5 with 5, 3.

If a player scores a hit he must be told what sort of ship he has struck. This enables him to search systematically if, for instance, he hits a battleship, as he must hit every part of that ship before it is sunk. The first player to sink the fleet of the other is the winner.

94

Materials. Graph paper (not essential).

Experiences to be gained. Number.

A square (or rectangle) is marked out as for a crossword puzzle and suitable clues are provided. This should be done by the children whenever possible and after checking by the teacher the puzzles can be exchanged.

The following example was made up by a group of eight-year-old boys.

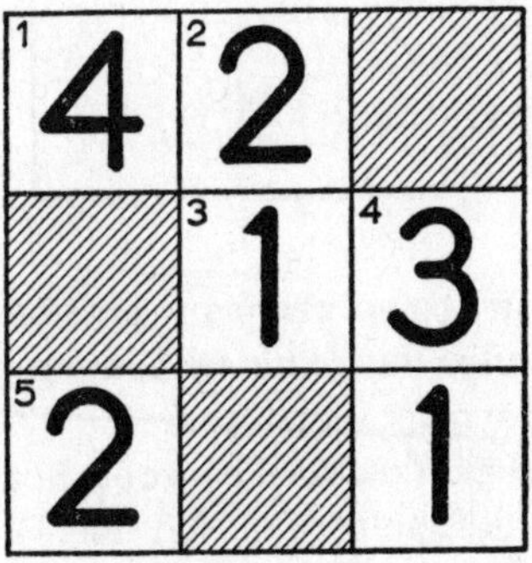

ACROSS.

1. It can be divided by 7 and by 3.
3. This number is unlucky.
5. A pair.

DOWN.

2. One more and there would be enough for two football teams.
4. A prime number.

The clues often lead to several answers, as in 4 Down, but the children decided they would then accept other answers provided they agreed with the clues.

95

Materials. None.

Experiences to be gained. Direction; use of units; vocabulary—left, right, up, down.

A square is divided into four smaller squares and any two of the nine points marked are used as the starting and finishing points. Two players are required and each draws, or is provided with, the figures described. We will suppose they decide to start at H and finish at C.

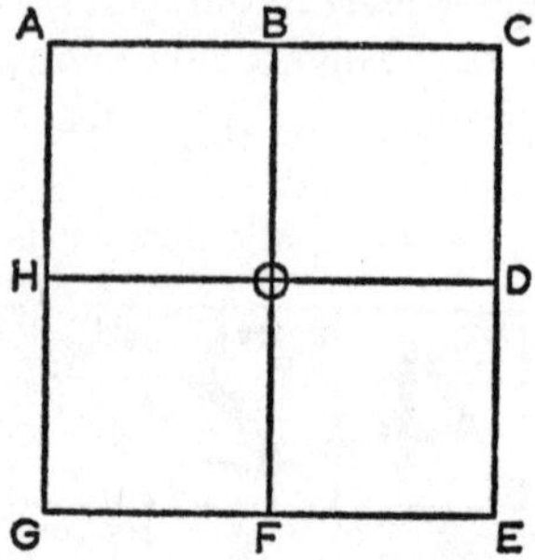

A player draws any one of the many possible routes from H to C. He then has to describe this route, without any of the letters, so that the second player can mark it on his sheet.

An eight-year-old girl described her route in this way:

'Start at the middle point of the left side.
Go down one unit then two units to the right.
Now go up two units and that's the end of the journey.'

Some children introduced compass directions and specified distances such as one mile, one inch, etc., even though the original square was not of the measurements they stated.

Geo-boards could be used instead of paper and pencil; graph paper enables the figures to be produced quickly and accurately.

96

Materials. Card.

Experiences to be gained. Classifying; shapes and their properties.

The following shapes could be presented to children, a red square, a blue right-angled triangle and two equilateral triangles—one blue and one red. Numerous variations of shape, colour, size, etc., would do just as well as those chosen, and these other possibilities should be used fully in subsequent games.

The object is to classify the set of figures in as many ways as possible, stating the reason for the classification each time.

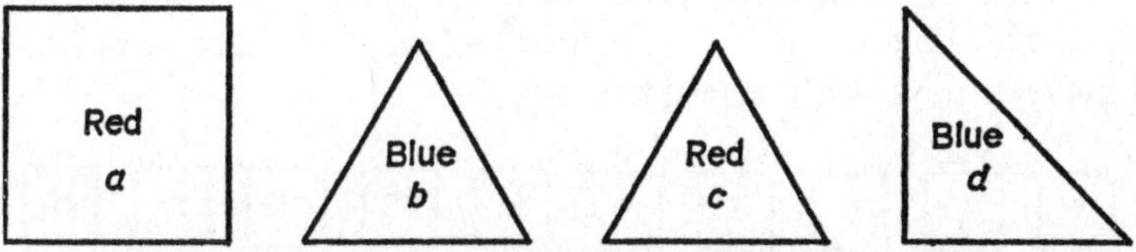

In the example chosen all the sides, except for the hypotenuse of the right-angled triangle, are equal in length (3 cm).

The following suggestions came from a group of children aged eight years. The figures have been coded for convenience (see diagram).

1. *a* and *c* (red); *b* and *d* (blue).
2. *a, b, c, d* all together (figures with a side 3 cm long).
3. *a, b, c, d* all together (figures with two sides the same length).
4. *a* and *d* (figures with a right angle); *b* and *c* (figures without a right angle).
5. *b, c* and *d* (figures with three sides); *a* (figure with more than three sides).

This caused an argument as some of the group insisted that a square has three sides—a nice logical point.

6. *a, b* and *c* (figures with all the sides equal in length); *d* (figure where all the sides are not equal in length).

The children then made other shapes and took it in turns to make particular groupings. The other children then had to say what the basis of classification was.

97

Materials. Thin card; scissors.

Experiences to be gained. Odd and even numbers; addition; number patterns and relationships.

Twenty houses or rectangles to represent them, are cut out of card and the numerals 1 to 20 written on them.

The children are asked to arrange the cards to represent a street. If they fail to place the odd numerals on one side and the even ones on the other, then the following activities should be postponed until the children have observed the arrangement of numerals in streets near their home or school. The use of the terms 'up' and 'down' the street should be discussed with the children and an arrow used to indicate whichever direction is agreed to be up.

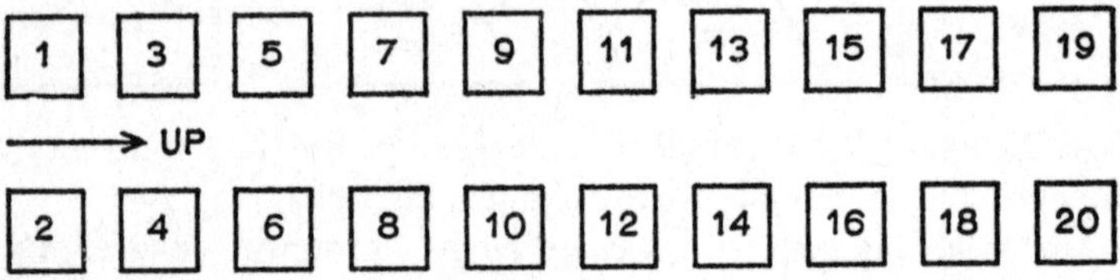

The children should be encouraged to construct questions and then exchange them. The following were suggested by a group of eight-year-olds.

Who lives opposite Number 13?

(They did not allow the child answering to look at the cards.)

How many houses are farther down the street than Number 10?

(There was a heated discussion as to whether the answer was four or eight but it was finally agreed that eight was the best answer.)

If the numbers on a pair of opposite houses add up to 23 what do the next pair higher up the street add up to?

Some seven-year-old children noted the following relationships: There are odd numbers on one side and even numbers on the other. The odd number in any pair of opposite houses is one smaller than the even number. If the opposite numbers are added they increase by four as you go up the street. The opposite ones, when added, always give an odd number.

Other questions and relationships emerged and led to additional investigations including the general properties of odd and even numbers.

98

Materials. Graph paper; counters.

Experiences to be gained. Introduction to co-ordinates; addition; recording.

The game is for two players. A square is cut out of graph paper, the size depending on the ability of the children.

1	2		3
	9	4	
8			
		5	

Numerals are written in some of the spaces.

One player (A) indicates a column (say the 2nd) and the other indicates a row (say the 3rd). The second player (B) has thus chosen the square with 9 in it and hence he records this as his score.

If each player is given a counter to place by the column and row selected they can ensure that no repetitions occur, i.e. any one row (or column) is used only once in a game. This is, of course, by no means essential.

The players take it in turn to play first so that in the game above B selects a column (say the 3rd) and A could then score 5 if he selects the first row.

Variations can be obtained by changing some, or all of the following: (a) the size of square played on, (b) the numerals (or number bonds) written in the small squares, (c) the rules of play. The children will suggest many other possibilities.

99

Materials. Ten rods, spills or strips of paper with graduated lengths from 1 cm to 10 cm. They should all be the same colour and thickness.

Experiences to be gained. Ordering; estimation of lengths.

One player removes a rod when the other is not looking and the remaining rods are thoroughly mixed. The task is to find, without moving any of the rods, the length of the missing rod. This will prove difficult for all except the older and more able children but can be simplified if the child is allowed to arrange the rods in order.

An alternative is to ask for the rod 1 cm shorter and also the one 1 cm longer than the missing rod.

If Cuisenaire rods are used the problem is easier as it can be solved by memory of the colours. It does however give practice in remembering the colours and their order.

100

Materials. Graph paper.

Experiences to be gained. Paper folding; symmetry; repeated patterns (similar figures).

A strip of graph paper (about 32 cm by 10 cm is a convenient size) is provided for each child.

This is folded in half (16 cm by 10 cm), then halved again (8 cm by 10 cm), and then again (4 cm by 10 cm). The work that arises from this is interesting in its own right but is not our immediate concern.

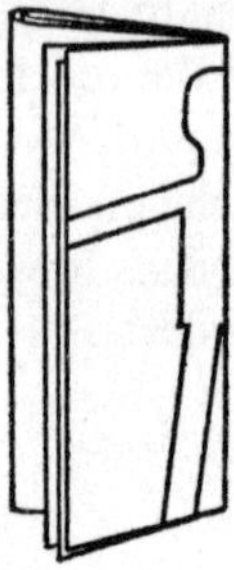

Half of a symmetrical figure is then drawn as shown, making sure it reaches to the edge of the paper. The figure is then cut out and the paper opened to give a chain of similar figures.

Christmas decorations can be made by modifying the figure to be cut out.

Many interesting questions will arise from this work. Here are a few examples.

What happens if the figure does not reach to the edge of the paper?

If we had cut out a semicircle what would have been the result?

The answer should say what shape the resulting figure would be as well as how many of them there will be.

101

Materials. None.

Experiences to be gained. Number appreciation; odd, even; division and other operations.

Any number of children can play.

One child is asked to think of a number that is between some agreed limits, and the others have to find it by asking questions. These must be of a form that can be answered by 'Yes', or 'No'.

Let us suppose the chosen number is thirty. The children take it in turn to ask questions, and a sequence from a class of eight-year-olds is given to illustrate the game.

(a) Is it more than fifty?	No.
(b) Is it an even number?	Yes.
(c) Will it divide exactly by three?	Yes.
(d) Is it more than twenty?	Yes.
(e) Is it twenty-four?	No.
(f) Is it forty-eight?	No.
(g) Is the first number a three?	Yes.
(h) Is it thirty-three?	No.
(i) Is it thirty?	Yes.

A reply of 'Yes' always produced an enthusiastic cheer whereas 'No' resulted in groans of disappointment. This was despite the fact that often the one gave as much information as the other.

Children are perhaps conditioned to associate 'Yes' with correctness and praise and the 'No' with wrong answers and humiliation. A lack of appreciation of the useful information gained is apparent in such reactions.

Early guesses such as (e) are soon condemned, but when they occasionally give the right answer children tend to use that strategy more frequently.

What is the best strategy to adopt?

102

Materials. Card.

Experiences to be gained. Addition; subtraction; division; multiplication.

The children each make up equations such as $7 - 2 + 1 = 6$. These are checked by the teacher and then written on the blackboard with the signs omitted, 7 2 1 6. The children then have to decide on a correct positioning of signs.

Provided the signs chosen give a correct equation it need not be necessarily the same as the child setting the problem had intended. Hence $7 = 2 - 1 + 6$ is a correct solution.

The more able children can be asked to find as many solutions as possible each time.

Difficulties about the order of the operations can be avoided by the use of brackets.

103

Materials. Duplicated plans of the classroom showing the tables or desks.

Experiences to be gained. Direction; simple co-ordinate ideas.

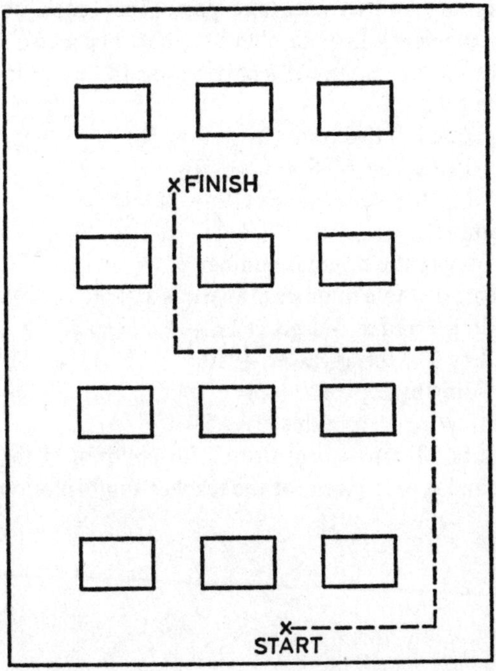

The desks or tables should be arranged in a regular pattern. The teacher, or a child, moves around the desks and the children mark in the route. One such route is shown on the diagram.

After checking the results a great deal of discussion will be needed. By using pencils of different colours the plans can be used a number of times.

A verbal description of the routes should be attempted and words such as row, column, left, right, back, forward, etc., will be required in addition to numbers.

104

Materials. None.

Experiences to be gained. Addition; division by 2; subtraction; number interest.

Any number of children can take part. They each write down a number and the next whole number above it. These two numbers are added together. For example if a child chose 14 he would add 14 and 15 and hence get 29.

Nine is now added to this total ($29 + 9 = 38$)

The result is divided by 2 ($38 \div 2 = 19$)

The original number is subtracted ($19 - 14 = 5$)

The final number is always 5

Proof: Let us call the original number x.
The next whole number above x is $x + 1$.
Adding x and $x + 1$ gives $2x + 1$.
Adding 9 to this gives $2x + 10$.
Dividing by 2 gives $x + 5$.
Subtracting x from this gives 5.

This proof is, of course, unsuitable for children of the age we are considering and is only given for the teacher's information.

105

Materials. None. (A geo-board could be used.)

Experiences to be gained. Shape, space and area.

A square is divided into sixteen smaller squares as shown. The figure

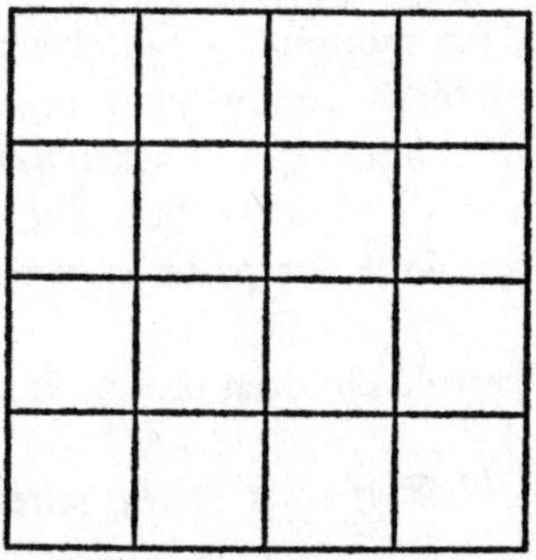

can be regarded as a cake that must be shared amongst four people so that each of them has the same amount of cake. The pieces must be the same shape and each portion in a complete piece.

As many solutions as possible should be found and not just the simple cases such as:

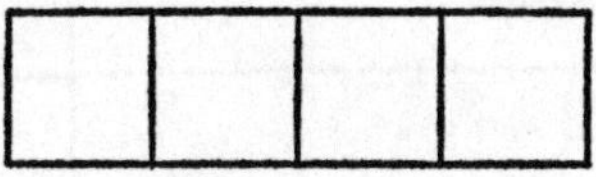

and

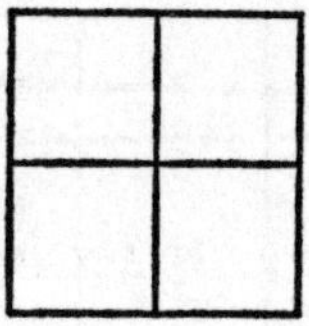

The original shape of the cake and number of people who are to share it can be varied.

106

Materials. Cuisenaire rods.

Experiences to be gained. Length equivalence; partitioning; patterns; recording.

Key:—*w* white; *r* red; *g* light green; *p* pink; *y* yellow.

Consider any rod, for example, a light green one. An equivalent length can be made up by the following arrangements: *w w w; w r; r w; g.* The children can be asked to find as many arrangements as possible for this and other rods. The older children should record their results and look for patterns in the equivalent number relations.

A group of nine-year-old children produced the following table:

Number of rods in the patterns

Colour of rod	One rod	Two rods	Three rods	Four rods	Five rods
w	*w*				
r	*r*	*ww*			
g	*g*	*rw; wr*	*www*		
p	*p*	*gw; wg; rr*	*rww; wrw; wwr*	*wwww*	
y	*y*	*wp; pw; rg; gr*	*gww; wgw; wwg; rrw; rwr; wrr*	*wwwr; wwrw; wrww; rwww*	*wwwww*

These results were then replaced by numbers:

Number of rods in the patterns

Length of rod in cm	One rod	Two rods	Three rods	Four rods	Five rods	Total
1	1					1
2	1	1				2
3	1	2	1			4
4	1	3	3	1		8
5	1	4	6	4	1	16

They decided the work could be extended by using the number patterns in the rows, columns and diagonals (Pascal's Triangle). The connection with partitioning was also noted, e.g. 3 can be represented as $1+1+1$; $2+1$; $1+2$ or 3 giving four possibilities. This corresponds to the third row of the last table.

107

Materials. Two dice.

Experiences to be gained. Addition; multiplication.

Each player takes it in turn to throw. He adds the two numbers indicated, then he multiplies them; the two results are added for his total score.

For example if he throws a 4 and a 5 he will score $9 + 20$ giving a total score for that throw of 29.

This game will be for the older children, but modifications such as only using addition (or only multiplication) can be introduced to suit the individual child.

108

Materials. Graph paper with small squares.

Experiences to be gained. Vocabulary—large, big, tall, etc.; proportion; area.

Each child draws a man (or any other figure), but the main lines must follow those printed on the graph paper.

A variety of questions can now arise and these should be answered in a concrete fashion by the children drawing. Children suggested the following when asked to bring in two, double or twice into a problem about the man they had drawn.

Draw a man that is twice as big.
Draw a man with double the height.
Draw a man two times as large.
Draw a man twice as tall.

They found that a figure twice as tall, but with the width unchanged, was not the same shape as the original. An appreciation of the ambiguous nature of words, like big, was soon developed, and a consequent need for more precise terms. When all the lengths were doubled they were surprised to find that the head became four times its original area.

With older children an investigation of cubes or cuboids would lead to the discovery that doubling all lengths would produce eight times the volume.

109

Materials. Two squares the same size, preferably with one transparent.

Experiences to be gained. Counting; spatial combinations; recording.

One square is placed on top of another, and the number of meeting points or intersections noted.

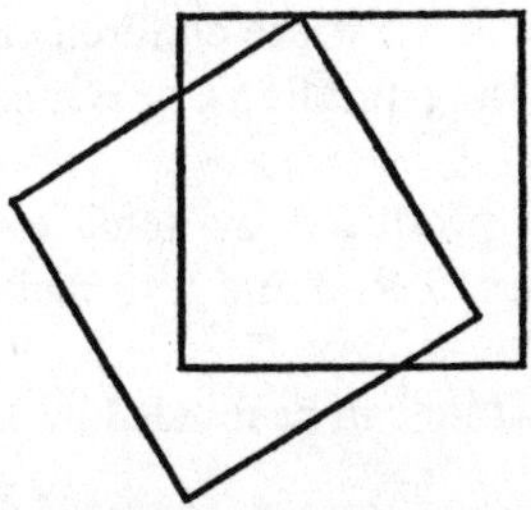

In the above there are three such points.

The children should now find examples where the number of meeting points is 1, 2 and so on.

What is the largest number of meeting points that can be made?

Can one make an example of every number up to the largest?

The results can be recorded by using gummed squares or by drawings.

Similar investigations could be carried out with other shapes.

110

Materials. None.

Experiences to be gained. Addition; subtraction; multiplication; division; odd and even numbers.

Each child provides a four-figure number. Suppose one child has 5436. Questions can be constructed by the child and these then set to the other children. Alternatively the teacher can set the questions, but this should only be done if the children cannot themselves produce a variety of interesting questions, or if some specific aspect needs to be emphasized.

The following were produced by some eight-year-old children.

Use the four numbers, 5, 4, 3 and 6 to make some odd numbers.

(3, 5, 53, 63, 45, etc.)

Make some numbers that can be divided by 3.

(3, 6, 45, 63, etc.)

Use all four figures to make two numbers so that when they are subtracted the answer is thirteen.

(56–43.)

Many more will be suggested by the children.

111

Materials. None.

Experiences to be gained. Addition; subtraction; multiplication; division.

This game is for the older and more able children. Using only the number four the children try to make as many other numbers as possible. They can use as many fours as they wish.

Some examples are $\frac{4}{4} = 1$

$$4 - \frac{4}{4} - \frac{4}{4} = 2$$

$$\frac{(4 \times 4) - 4}{4} = 3$$

Credit can be given for originality at some children may discover that they can get any number by adding the requisite number of $\frac{4}{4}$ s.

For example for 5 they might write $\frac{4}{4}+\frac{4}{4}+\frac{4}{4}+\frac{4}{4}+\frac{4}{4}$.

Numbers other than four could be used and a limit could be placed on how many of each are used, e.g. four 4s or five 5s.

This game is particularly suited to team competitions.

112

Materials. None.

Experiences to be gained. Division; number appreciation.

By saving the ends of candles until he has ten of them, a man can melt them down and thus make one candle.

If he starts with 100 candles how many can he burn altogether?

Answer. From the 100 ends he can make a further 10 candles. The 10 ends will enable him to make another candle, so he can burn 111.

113

Materials. Three rods and a block of wood; rings. (Cuisenaire rods can be used instead of this material.)

Experiences to be gained. Size; mental imagery; counting; sequence and patterns of actions.

This game is for one player. The rods are inserted into the wood and the rings placed over one of the rods so that they decrease in size towards the top.

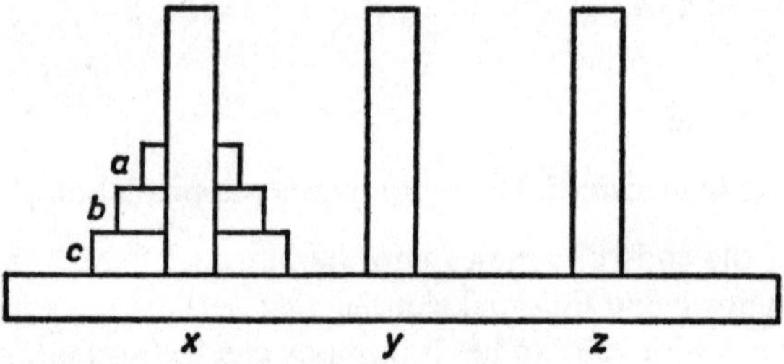

The object is to transfer the rings from one rod to another, moving only one ring at a time, so that they finish in the same relative positions as they started. At no time must a ring be placed on top of a smaller one. If the rings are denoted by *a*, *b*, and *c* and the rods by *x*, *y*, and *z* as shown in the diagram, the following sequence might take place:

(⟶ denotes 'moves to')

(1) $a \longrightarrow y$ (2) $b \longrightarrow z$ (3) $a \longrightarrow z$
(4) $c \longrightarrow y$ (5) $a \longrightarrow x$ (6) $b \longrightarrow y$
(7) $a \longrightarrow y$

This has taken seven moves. Can it be done in fewer moves? The children can then investigate the situation when there are four rings. The rhythm and pattern involved can often be established when the children are too young to explain or record their method of working.

114

Materials. None.

Experiences to be gained. Addition; subtraction; place value.

The following are suitable for older children who are already familiar with the addition of two digit numbers.

A question such as the following is set to the children:

$$\begin{array}{r} A\,4 \\ +1\,A \\ \hline X\,9 \\ \hline \end{array}$$

Find what number A stands for and also what number is missing from the place marked X.

If the children fail to do this even when working in groups more practice with the addition of two digit numbers may be needed. Questions such as, 'What must be added to 4 if the result is 9?' should be sufficient to lead to a solution. A stands for 5 and the missing number that X stands for is 6. The younger children can be introduced to this work by simple problems such as '4 added to a certain number makes 9' or

$$\begin{array}{r} 4 \\ +\ A \\ \hline 9 \\ \hline \end{array}$$

Find A.

A mapping notation could be used if the children are familiar with it

$(4, A) \longrightarrow 9$

The children should make up similar problems of their own and exchange them with each other.

Subtraction and other operations could be introduced as well as addition.

For example

$$\begin{array}{r} 2\,3 \\ \times\ \ B \\ \hline 69 \\ \hline \end{array}$$

115

Materials. None.

Experiences to be gained. Counting; number sequences; parallel lines.

Two lines are drawn to cross at one point. A third line is drawn to intersect the other two. A fourth line is drawn to intersect the other three and the results are recorded:

2 lines cross in 1 point (at the most)

3 lines cross in 3 points (at the most)

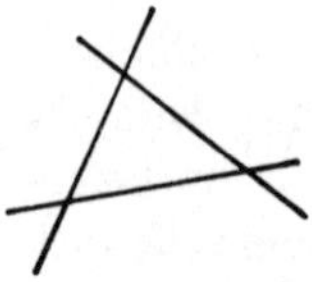

4 lines cross in 6 points (at the most)

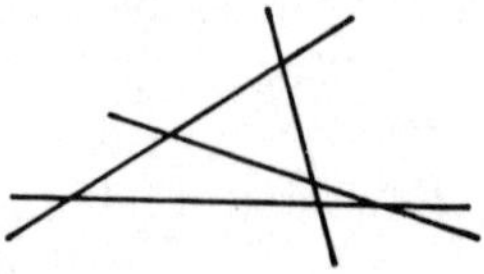

5 lines cross? (at the most)

The sequence can be extended, first by actually drawing the lines and counting the points of intersection and later by observing the pattern of the recorded sequences.

The older children will appreciate the need for the reservation that the recorded intersections are 'at the most' as parallel lines might be involved and thus reduce the number of intersecting points.

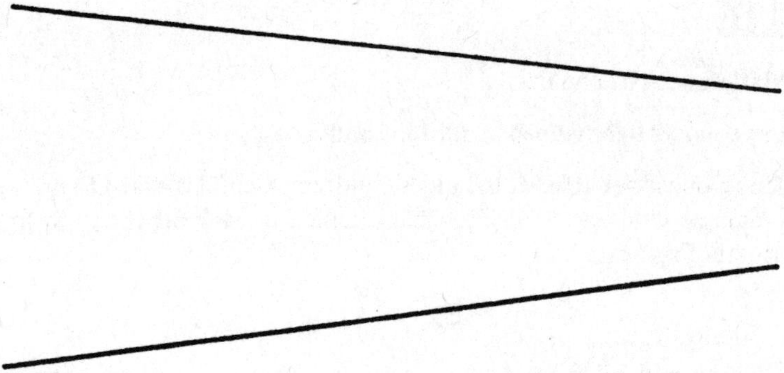

The case of lines that are not parallel, yet fail to meet on the sheet of paper used (see above) may cause some difficulty and this case will need careful introduction and discussion.

116

Materials. A calendar.

Experiences to be gained. Addition; multiplication.

This game is suitable for the older children. A child is asked to draw a square around any four dates that are next to each other and form a square. For example:

13	14	or	22	23
20	21		29	30

These will all form two pairs of consecutive numbers with the lower ones each seven more than the ones above them. The children should be encouraged to find these and other relationships, but if they cannot the following sort of problems could be set:

(a) Multiply the smallest number by 4 and add 16 to the result. Do this for several sets of numbers. What do you notice? (The result is the total of the four numbers each time. Why?)

(b) Add the diagonally opposite numbers. What do you notice? (The totals are always the same.)
Can you explain why?

Other sets of numbers could be investigated, for example any four numbers that are situated at the corners of a square, e.g.

5	–	–	8
–	–	–	–
19	–	–	22

Three of these might be given and the fourth found by the children. Many other relationships will emerge from the children's own discoveries and these will be far more valuable than specific tasks set by the teacher.

117

Materials. None.

Experiences to be gained. Addition.

Some lines are drawn all crossing at the same point. The problem is to write the numerals 1 to 8 at the ends of the lines so that the sum of each pair of numbers is the same.

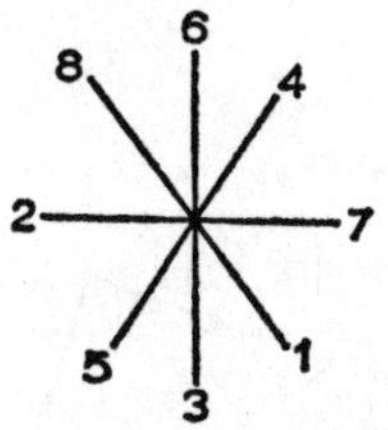

It will be noticed that the sum of each such pair is one more than the last numeral, in the given case they therefore add up to 9. This result should be discovered by the children if possible. The number of lines drawn initially can be varied, but will always involve an even number of numerals.

If an odd number is required, say 11, the middle number 6 can be placed at the point where the lines cross, as shown below.

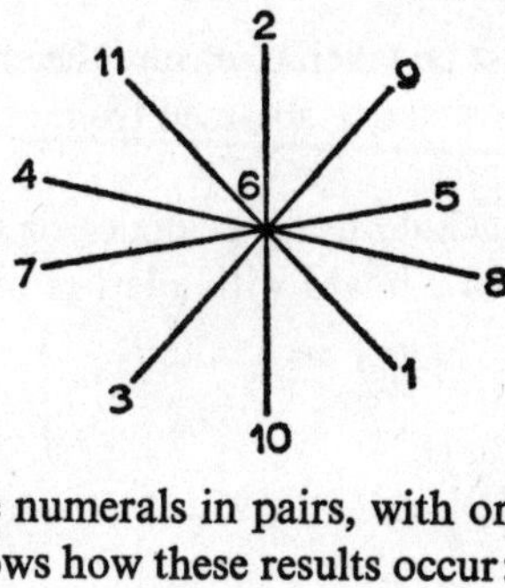

The linking of the numerals in pairs, with one decreasing and the other increasing, shows how these results occur:

1 opposite 11
2 opposite 10
3 opposite 9
4 opposite 8
5 opposite 7.

118

Materials. Geo-board; rubber bands.

Experiences to be gained. Squares; right angles; rotation; translation.

The object is to make as many different-sized squares as possible. Some children will need assistance if they fail to suggest any 'skew' cases such as the ones shown below. Two squares the same size do

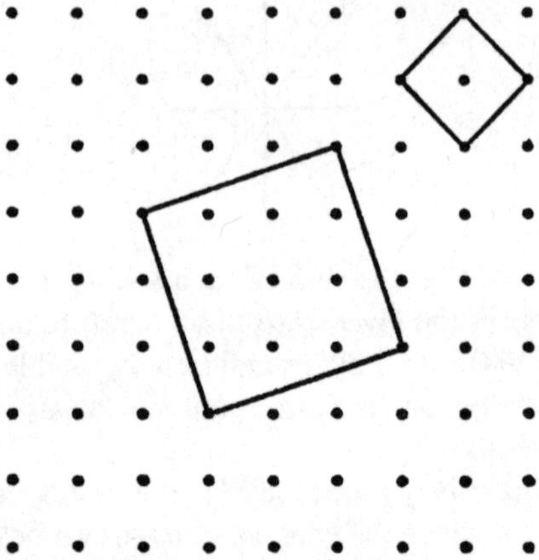

not count so care must be taken to ensure the children appreciate the equivalence of figures that are obtained from others by rotation and/or translation.

Variations could include using triangles or rectangles instead of squares and playing on a board with a lattice of equilateral triangles (isometric).

119

Materials. None.

Experiences to be gained. Number patterns and relationships.

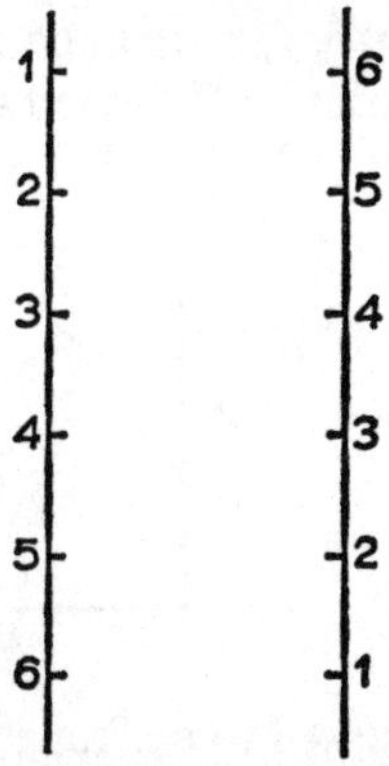

The children draw or are provided with the diagram above. They can then join the points in any meaningful way they wish, recording and commenting on their results.

This should result in many interesting discoveries. For example:

(a) By joining pairs of the same numerals the lines form crosses. All the crosses meet at the same point.

(b) By joining points horizontally the pairs of numbers each total seven.

(c) By using more than six numerals the totals in (b) can be increased.

(d) If we join the numbers giving a total of five we get two sets of parallel lines. This can also be done with numbers other than five.

(e) If we introduce zero and negative numbers the idea in (d) can be extended.

(f) We could make investigations with both sets of numbers increasing in the same direction.

(g) Even numbers could be written on one line and odd numbers on the other. Many other variations can be found by the children and the teacher.

120

Materials. None.

Experiences to be gained. Addition; number combinations.

The numerals 1, 2, 3, 4, 5, 6, 7, 8 are to be written round the sides of a square so that the three numbers on each side total 12.

Solution

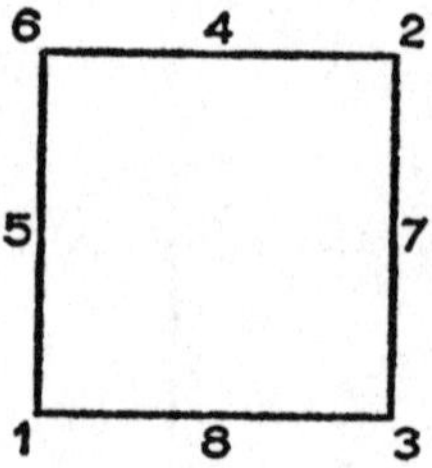

The children are then asked to rearrange them so the totals are 13 instead of 12. Similarly they can make the totals 14 and 15.

Possible solutions for 13, 14 and 15 respectively are as follows:

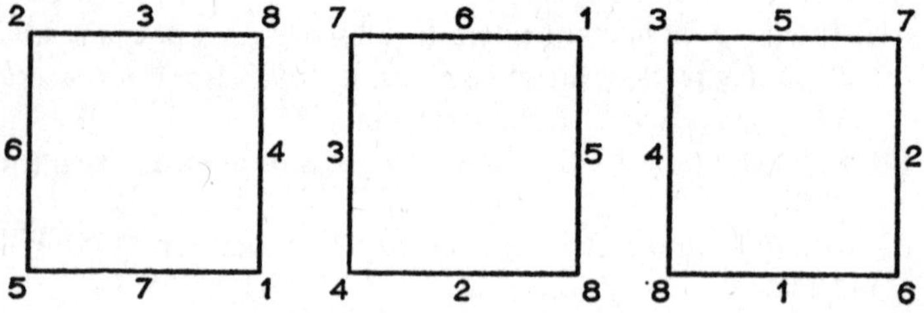

121

Materials. None.

Experiences to be gained. Addition; multiplication; cubes.

$$\begin{array}{c} 1 \\ 3 + 5 \\ 7 + 9 + 11 \end{array}$$

What do you think the next line will be? Why?

(13 + 15 + 17 + 19 because there are 1, 2 and then 3 odd numbers in the previous lines so the next will be the next 4 odd numbers.)

Write down the next line also. 21 + 23 + 25 + 27 + 29

The children now add the numbers in each line and look for other patterns and relationships. This might result in

$$\begin{array}{ccrcl} 1 & = & 1 & = & 1 \times 1 \times 1 \\ 3 + 5 & = & 8 & = & 2 \times 2 \times 2 \\ 7 + 9 + 11 & = & 27 & = & 3 \times 3 \times 3 \\ 13 + 15 + 17 + 19 & = & 64 & = & 4 \times 4 \times 4 \\ 21 + 23 + 25 + 27 + 29 & = & 125 & = & 5 \times 5 \times 5 \end{array}$$

The older children might wish to continue the series. The notation 1^3, 2^3, 3^3, etc., could be introduced.

They may notice that successive subtraction of terms gives 7, 19, 37, 61. These are all prime numbers.

Would this still be true if we took more terms of the series?

122

Materials. None.

Experiences to be gained. Addition; subtraction.

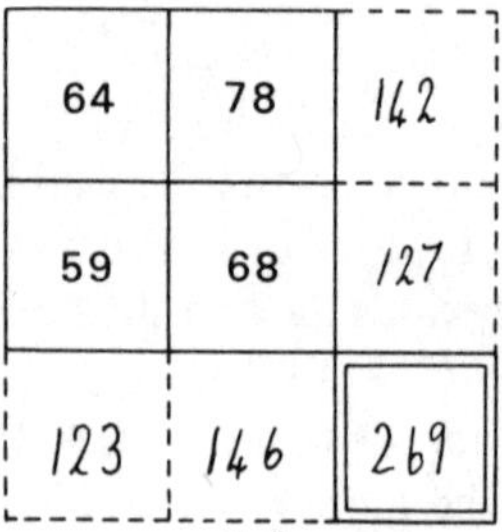

(a)

Four numbers are placed in the cells as shown (64, 78, 59, 68). The totals are then entered for the two rows and the two columns, i.e. 142, 127, 123 and 146.

The 269 is then found from 142 + 127 and 123 + 146 so the work is self-checking.

The numbers can be adjusted to allow for varying abilities ranging from single digits up to decimal and vulgar fractions.

Subtraction is practised when some of the sub-totals are given instead of the four numbers as in (*a*)

For example.

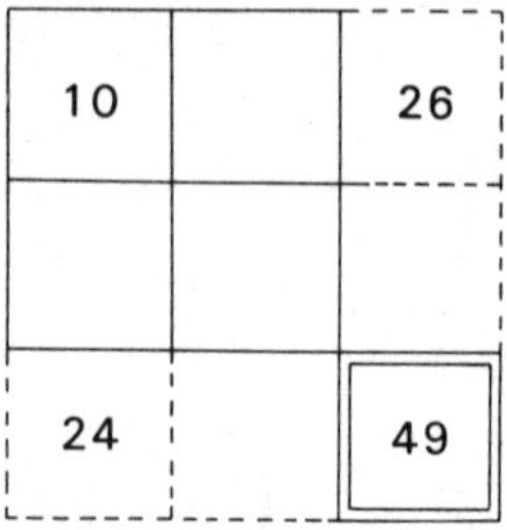

(b)

A similar diagram could be used for multiplication.

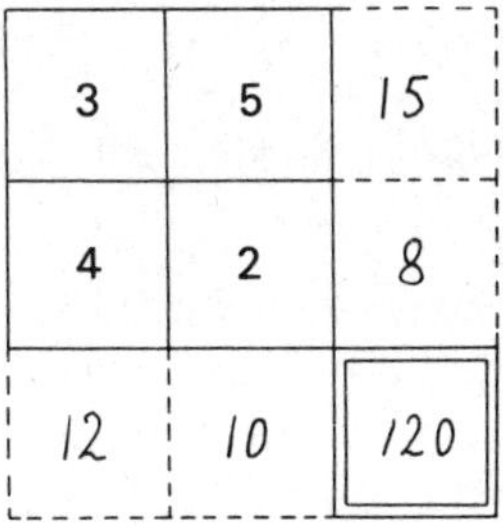

(c)

123

Materials. Forty cards as described below.

Experiences to be gained. Practice of multiplication facts; memorising.

This activity is illustrated for the tables of 4 but any other tables could be practised in a similar way. Two or more players can take part.

Forty cards are needed, four for each of the numbers 1 to 10.

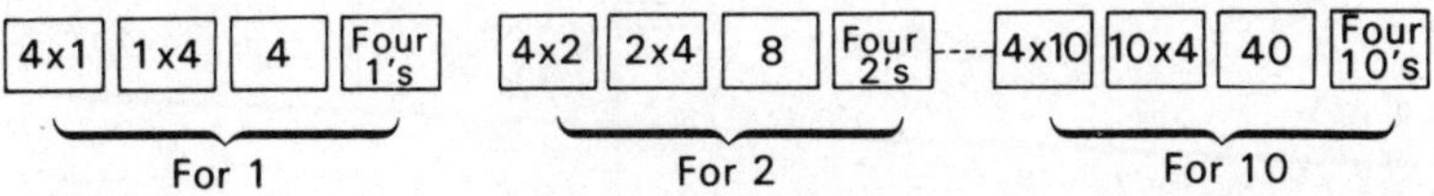

A special case arises when 4 is used and then the cards should be

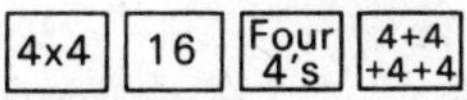

The forty cards are shuffled and placed face downwards in four rows with ten cards in each row, or any other arrangement if preferred. The first player turns over two cards so that everyone can see them clearly. If the cards represent the same number he keeps them and has another turn. Otherwise the cards are turned face downwards again.

The second player then does the same and so on in turn until all the cards have been taken. The player with the most cards at the end is the winner.

124

Materials. A set of ten cards: [1] [2] [3] [4] [5] [6] [7] [8] [9] [10]

Experiences to be gained. Practice in multiplication; addition; subtraction.

The game is for two players who should sit side by side. The cards are shuffled and placed in a pile face downwards. Any of the multiplication tables could be practised. 8 is used to illustrate the method.

Player A turns over the top card (6), multiplies the number on it by 8 and records the score (48). The second player B does the same (5) and records his score (40). A and B continue to turn cards alternately until all ten cards have been used. The player with the highest total score wins.

	A	B
	48	40
	16	24
	80	72
	8	32
	56	64
Total	208	232

To practise subtraction each player starts with 400 and subtracts his score each time. In the game above, for his first turn

A would calculate

$$\begin{array}{r} 400 \\ -\ 48 \\ \hline 352 \\ \hline \end{array}$$

B would calculate

$$\begin{array}{r} 400 \\ -\ 40 \\ \hline 360 \\ \hline \end{array}$$

This continues for the other turns and the player finishing with the lower number wins.

The starting number need not be 400 but should not be less than 320. Why?

125

Materials. Two sets, each with ten cards:

1	2	3	4	5	6	7	8	9	10

Experiences to be gained. Practice in multiplication; addition; subtraction.

This game is for two players, A and B, who should sit side by side.

Shuffle each set of cards separately.

Place them, face downwards, next to each other.

Player A turns over the top two cards and multiplies the numbers on them ($8 \times 4 = 32$).

8	4

B then does the same ($1 \times 6 = 6$) and play continues alternately until all cards are used.

The results could be recorded as follows.

A	B
8x4 = 32	1x6 = 6
2x5 = 10	10x7 = 70
3x2 = 6	7x3 = 21
6x9 = 54	9x1 = 9
4x10 = 40	5x8 = 40
Total = 142	Total = 146

The player with the greater total wins.

To practise subtraction players start with a number (not less than 330) and subtract each score successively.

The player with the lower score wins.

Alternatives:

The sums or differences could be used instead of the products.

126

Materials. None.

Experiences to be gained. Addition; subtraction; multiplication; division.

Codes can provide practice in any one of the four operations or in a combination of them.

The example below is limited to multiplication and division.

To construct a code first decide on a message.

MATHS GAMES ARE FUN.

Draw one box for each letter and with a gap between the words.

M	A	T	H	S		G	A	M	E	S
24x3	48÷6	24÷2	39÷3	1.5x6		5x8	80÷10	8x9	64÷4	10x9

A	R	E		F	U	N
56÷7	14x7	80÷5		180÷9	12x8	29x3

Write a suitable clue under the first box. $24 \times 3 = 72$ so 72 stands for M. The M in GAMES must also be 72 so it could be 8×9. The first A has $48 \div 6$ under it so must be 8. The A's in GAMES and ARE must therefore also come to 8.

All the other letters used are decided in a similar manner. The remaining letters of the alphabet can then be given any numbers at all. Naturally the letters are omitted from the boxes when presented to the pupils.

For example

A	B	C	D	E	F	G	H	I	J	K	L	M
8	11	23	30	16	20	40	13	52	63	9	34	72

N	O	P	Q	R	S	T	U	V	W	X	Y	Z
87	37	81	79	98	90	12	96	76	56	19	45	27

127

Materials. None.

Experiences to be gained. Addition; subtraction; multiplication; division; adding fractions.

4	9	2
3	5	7
8	1	6

(a)

In the usual form of magic square the numbers are consecutive, starting at 1.

Variations of this theme provide valuable arithmetic practice.

The totals for rows, columns and diagonals must all be the same.

What happens if 4 is added to each number in (*a*)? Is the result a magic square?

By how much have the totals been increased?

8	13	6
7	9	11
12	5	10

(b)

The total is increased by 12 since three 4's have been added. Pupils can be led to the general rule that if a number n is added the total is increased by $3n$.

Subtracting 1 from each number in (*b*) results in a magic square.

How are the totals affected? This can be investigated when other numbers are subtracted.

Similarly pupils could divide each number by, say, 2 and see if they then get a magic square. This gives practice in adding fractions.

How are the totals affected?

128

Materials. None.

Experiences to be gained. Addition; halving; multiplication.

First give the pupils ten consecutive numbers and ask them to find their sum.

Suppose you chose $28 + 29 + 30 + 31 + 32 + 33 + 34 + 35 + 36 + 37$.

Most pupils will rewrite the numbers in vertical form but the more able ones could be encouraged to add them without rewriting, a far more difficult task.

They then add the first and last numbers

$$\begin{array}{r} 28 \\ +37 \\ \hline 65 \\ \hline \end{array}$$

There are ten numbers. Half of 10 is 5. Multiply 65 by 5.

$$\begin{array}{r} 65 \\ \times\ 5 \\ \hline 325 \\ \hline \end{array}$$

The sum of the ten numbers should also be 325.

They should repeat this for other sets of ten numbers.

If instead eight numbers had been used they would multiply the sum of the first and last numbers by 4.

If eleven numbers they would have multiplied by $5\frac{1}{2}$ and so on.

Formula $(\text{First term} + \text{last term}) \times \dfrac{\text{Number of terms}}{2}$

This works for any series in which the difference between consecutive terms is always the same.

$19 + 22 + 25 + 28 + 31 + 34 + 37 + 40$

$19 + 40 = 59$ Half of 8 is 4

$59 \times 4 = 236$. The total is therefore 236.

129

Materials. Bingo cards similar to those illustrated below. Counters.

Experiences to be gained. Addition; subtraction; multiplication; division.

This Bingo game is for three or more players, one acting as the 'caller'.

Each player is given a different card. The number facts used can be varied to suit the ability of the pupils and the operations that need practising.

The illustrated cards are confined to multiplication and division within the tables for 2, 3, 4 and 5.

4x5	5x8	24÷3
7x3	4x9	2x7
9x2	45÷5	16÷2

2x3	5x6	9x4
18÷2	10x5	2x6
4x7	20÷4	3x3

9x3	27÷3	3x4
40÷4	8x4	5x4
4x10	7x5	8x2

3x5	4x3	5x7
28÷4	9x5	2x4
10x2	30÷3	8x3

The 'caller' is provided with small cards numbered 1 to 100 but play will be speeded up if numbers that are not on any cards are removed. In this instance 31, 47, 77, etc., could be omitted. It must first be agreed as to what constitutes a win, completing a row, column, diagonal or else the whole card. The players place counters on the cards as the corresponding numbers are called. The winning line (or card) must be checked against the numbers called.

The procedure could be reversed with the caller's cards containing the operations (e.g. 4 × 5) and the players' cards the numerals (20).

130

Materials. A set of five cards marked [1] [2] [3] [4] [5]

Experiences to be gained. Division; odd and even; permutations.

The object is to make 2-digit numbers with the cards and score as many points as you can in, say, five minutes. The cards are replaced each time and can be used again and again.

1 point for an odd number.
2 points for an even number.
3 points for a number greater than 40.
4 points for a number that divides exactly by 3.
45 would score 1 (odd) + 3 (greater than 40) + 4 (divisible by 3) = 8.
If a player only claimed 1 + 3 he would score 4 instead of 8.
Other activities.

Play a similar game but with 3-digit numbers.
Find all the 20 possible 2-digit numbers.
Find all the 60 possible 3-digit numbers.
Change the given method of scoring.
Have more (or less) cards.

131

Materials. Six cards marked [1] [2] [3] [4] [5] [6]

Arrange the cards as shown to give a correct answer.

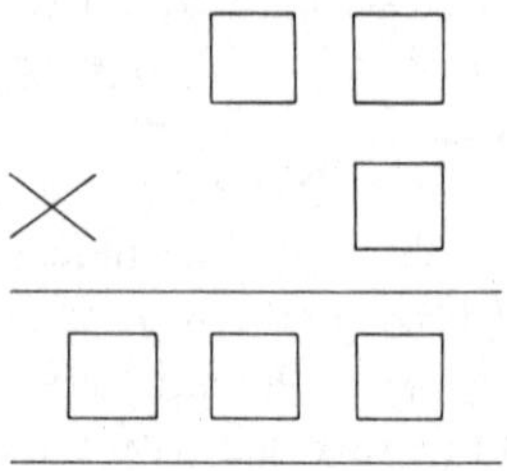

132

Materials. Prepare arrays of numbers similar to those illustrated below. Spirit master duplicated sheets are a convenient way of producing copies.

Experiences to be gained. Addition; subtraction; multiplication.

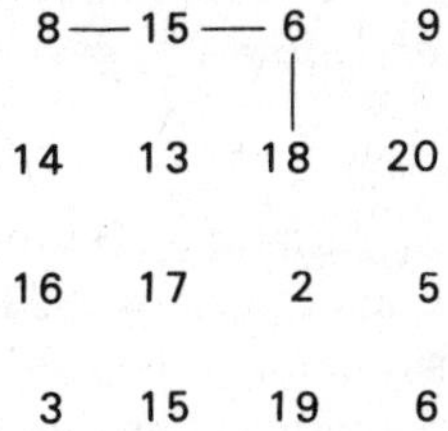

Any number can play. All the pupils work on the same array. A few examples of the many possible variations are now given.

(i) Join any four numbers by horizontal or vertical lines so that they form a chain. In the illustration above the score is $8 + 15 + 6 + 18 = 47$.
What is the highest possible score? What is the lowest possible score?

(ii) Change the number of links in the chain and play as in (i).

(iii) Ring round any two numbers that are next to one another, horizontally or vertically. Multiply them. Ring a second pair and multiply them. Add your two products together to obtain your score.

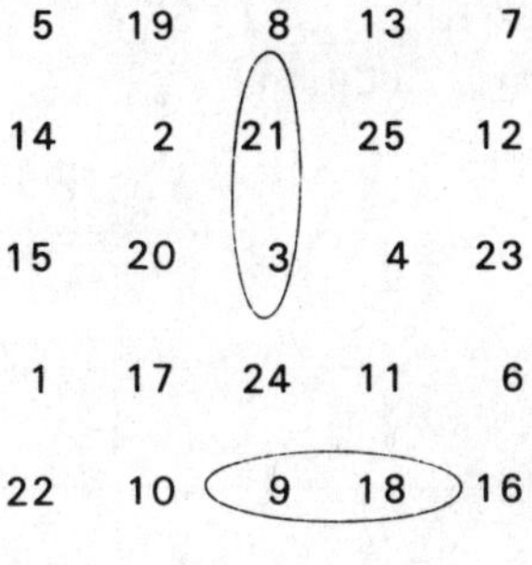

$21 \times 3 = 63,\quad 9 \times 18 = 162,\quad 63 + 162 = 225.$
What is the highest possible score? What is the lowest possible score? Can you score 121?

133

Materials. None.
Experiences to be gained. Multiplication; addition; subtraction.
Any number of players can take part. Each writes down their Christian name.

Under each letter they write a number according to the order of letters in the alphabet. A = 1, B = 2, C = 3, and so on up to Z = 26.

E.g.	B	E	T	T	Y
	2	5	20	20	25

There are many possible variations. Here are a few of them.

1. The greatest number is multiplied by the least. 25 × 2 = 50. The player with the highest number then wins.
2. The greatest number is multiplied by the second greatest. 25 × 20 = 500. Highest wins.
3. The numbers are all added. Highest total wins.
4. The least number is subtracted from the greatest. Highest (or lowest) wins.

Instead of Christian names towns, flowers, animals, etc., could be used.

134

Materials. Cards.

0 1 2 3 4 5 6 7 8 9

Experiences to be gained. Addition.

Arrange the ten cards so as to satisfy this sum:

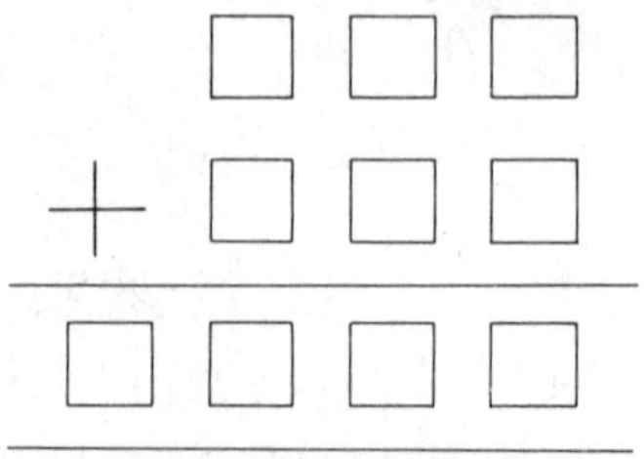

Can you find more than one solution?